GOPHER GLORY

The Pride of the Maroon & Gold

GOPHER GLORY

The Pride of the Maroon & Gold

JIM BRUTON

Cataloging-in-Publication Data is available from the Library of Congress.

First KCI Sports Publishing edition: 2009
ISBN-13: 978-0-9798729-7-6
ISBN-10: 0-9798729-7-9

Book Layout and Design: Nicky Brillowski

This book is available in quantity at special discounts for your group or organization. For further information, contact:

KCI Sports Publishing
3340 Whiting Avenue
Suite 5
Stevens Point, WI 54481
(217) 766-3390
Fax: (715) 344-2668

Photos courtesy of: Credits to Minnesota Athletic Communications, and Jeff Keiser-Creative Director, University of Minnesota.

CONTENTS

DEDICATION

From the time I was ten years old, my dad took me to every Minnesota Gophers football game. For the next nine seasons we lived and died with our maroon and gold, with the great national champions of 1960 and the Rose Bowl teams of 1961 and 1962.

I remember traveling to the games and sharing the excitement as we headed toward campus. I remember munching on hot dogs and reading every word in the game day "Gopher Goal Post" program before the Gophers ran out onto the field. Every moment was special. The best part was that we were able to share the great memories.

In 1965 and 1966, I was on the Minnesota Gophers squad and played in a couple of games. I have always wondered how dad felt when I kicked off against Indiana and made the tackle or when he took his seat on the sideline bench on "Dads Day." I never asked him.

Dad died 40 years ago this year and I miss him, more so every fall. Our time together was what dreams are made of. Dad loved the Gophers, cherishing every victory and barely enduring each loss. He taught me about family values and enjoying what you believe in. I wish he could see the new stadium and be there when the Gophers win the Big Ten Championship and return to the Rose Bowl.

This book, *GOPHER GLORY: The Pride of the Maroon and Gold,* is for you, dad.

Remember our great times? I miss you.

ACKNOWLEDGEMENTS

I want to express my deepest appreciation and sincere gratitude to Joel Maturi, athletic director at the University of Minnesota, and Tim Brewster, Minnesota Golden Gophers head football coach. Without their support and commitment to assisting me in writing *GOPHER GLORY: The Pride of the Maroon and Gold*, the book would never have become a reality. I also want to thank them for writing the Forewords for the book.

I would also like to express my thanks to associate athletic directors Tom Wistrcill and Marc Ryan, who have also endorsed and supported every aspect of the project and have been a pleasure to know.

Further, my sincere gratitude goes out to Meghan Potter and Dan O'Brien in Coach Brewster's office, Andy Seeley in Gopher Communications, and George Adzick, director of the "M" Club, who has each provided valuable assistance and meant more to the process than they will ever know. It has been my true pleasure getting to know each of them.

My special thanks also goes out to Peter Clark at KCI Sports Publishing, who has been great to work with and who has pledged his full support of the book.

Finally, as always, my deepest affection and thanks goes to my wonderful family who continues to provide me with their magnificent love and support.

-Jim Bruton

FOREWORD

If you are a fan of the Minnesota Golden Gophers football team, then *GOPHER GLORY: The Pride of the Maroon and Gold* is the book for you. It truly captures the great history and tradition of Gopher football beginning as far back as the 1800s and our first game ever played at the Minnesota State Fairgrounds against Hamline University.

Jim Bruton has put together a collection of incredible facts and memories in a passionately descriptive manner, highlighting the great Gopher teams and players of the past, from a loyal maroon and gold perspective. He has accentuated the greatness and history of Gopher football pride and traditions, allowing the reader to share in the excitement and passion.

Jim has it all covered in the book-the coaches, the players, the great All-Americans, the championships, Gopher voices, the captains, the new stadium and the entire concept of Minnesota football returning to campus. The book is an inspiring, heartfelt collection of facts, anecdotes and descriptions of over a century of Golden Gopher football-a must read!

-Joel Maturi
Director of Athletics
University of Minnesota

FOREWORD

As the 26th head football coach of the Minnesota Golden Gophers, I am a strong believer in the great traditions and history of Gopher football. I constantly reflect upon the incredible history of six national championships and 18 Big Ten titles made possible by the many great players who have worn the maroon and gold with pride.

Jim Bruton has truly captured the significance of it all, with great passion and pride. He brings us up close to the greatest coaches and players of the past: Bernie Bierman, Bronko Nagurski, "Pug" Lund, Bud Grant, Bruce Smith, Murray Warmath, Bobby Bell, Carl Eller, Sandy Stephens, and a host of others.

GOPHER GLORY: The Pride of the Maroon and Gold says it all, and is reflected in this loyal, dedicated and passionate tribute to the incredible history identified with Minnesota Golden Gophers football. I am humbled on a daily basis by the tradition and history that make the Gophers so special. This book allows you to walk with the legends and enjoy a very special journey of over a century of Gopher Glory.

-Tim Brewster
Head Coach
University of Minnesota

INTRODUCTION

Saturdays in the Fall

It was a beautiful brisk Saturday morning in mid-November. The brilliant fall colors in combination with the Gophers' traditional maroon and gold created a magnificent setting for a football game. But it wasn't going to be just any football game. It was University of Minnesota Golden Gopher football and it was magical.

My dad and I were on our way to Minneapolis and the University of Minnesota's Memorial Stadium, the home of our Golden Gophers.

When I was growing up in the mid 1950s every football Saturday had an emotional fervor to it. My routine was almost always the same. I would rise early, check the weather conditions, consume the sports pages to prepare for the day's game, and begin to feel the excitement and anticipation of the forthcoming afternoon of football.

It was a special feeling I had on those Saturdays. I'm not sure whether the players or even Coach Murray Warmath could have been more excited and nervous than I was as my dad and I headed for the University of Minnesota campus and the much-awaited kick off. At that time in my life, there were few things more important. I loved the Golden Gophers and everything about the team. Each Golden Gopher home game was a special time for me because I was able to enjoy the exploits of the great Gopher teams with my dad.

I was nine years old when I first started following Golden Gopher football, so I wouldn't be quarterbacking the Gophers those fall afternoons nor would I be running for a crucial first down or kicking the winning field goal. I wouldn't be catching a pass across the middle of the field and eluding tackles for the winning touchdown. I might as well have, though, because I truly lived each play.

INTRODUCTION

Dad taught me to love Gopher football from the first time we took in a game together during the 1954 season. From then on, we went to them all. For ten years we never missed a home game, through the sadness and dismay of the tumultuous times and the enormity and splendor of the glory years. When I wasn't in attendance, I listened intently on the radio. During the 1954 season, I became enamored with All-American Bob McNamara, the powerful fullback for the Golden Gophers. I still remember the Iowa game that year and the remarkable 22-20 victory. It didn't take long for me to fall in love with Gopher football, quickly identify the maroon and gold heroes, and revel in the excitement of those special autumn Saturdays.

Together we suffered the losses in the late 50s and although the sting of each loss hurt, in reality, it didn't matter. We were together on those special Saturdays and together we fulfilled our passion for Golden Gopher football.

One of the most memorable games was against Northwestern at Memorial Stadium on October 13, 1956 during a torrential rainstorm which lasted throughout the game. From the pre-game warm ups to the final gun, rain came down in buckets. But Dad and I suffered through it. What were we supposed to do; leave because it was a little wet outside? Abandon our Golden Gophers while they were doing battle? I don't think so.

And when the darkness of the afternoon fell upon us, the final score told the story of the kind of afternoon it was: Minnesota Gophers 0 and the Northwestern Wildcats 0. It was impossible to score. The players were soaked. The coaches were soaked. The fans were soaked. The field was a mess. But it didn't matter. It was Gopher football and we were there to take it all in.

As the years passed from the day I attended my first Gopher game, I had learned a little about team records, national rankings and game favorites, of which the Gophers usually held the underdog role. But once I felt the game day excitement at the stadium and watched our beloved Gophers take the field, stats and predictions really didn't matter. As far as I was concerned, Minnesota was always going to win!

This is a story about the maroon and gold—the past, present and future of great athletes, teams, and coaches who have and will honor Gopher football and the University of Minnesota traditions.

This is Golden Gopher football from inside this great University. This is a book about coaches, administrators and great athletes who have represented the University with the greatest of pride, commitment and passion. This is not a book just about football, THIS IS *GOPHER GLORY: THE PRIDE OF THE MAROON AND GOLD.*

1

TRADITION OF THE MAROON AND GOLD

"LOOK! RIGHT THERE ON THE WALL . . . . Bobby Bell and Carl Eller! They are arguably the two greatest defensive players to ever play the game ....who is going to argue with you about that?"

He said it with great pride. The power of his statement and the passion in his voice left no doubt of the greatness of these men, men of great stature, men who wore the maroon and gold.

Both Bell and Eller played at the University of Minnesota, both future college and professional football Hall of Famers. And when it comes to writing a book about the tradition of Golden Gopher football, it is only fitting to have a full chapter on the two. For those who have been loyal followers of Gopher greats, Bell and Eller says it all. The faithful will know.

Maybe the title of the chapter should just read "Bell and Eller" and the rest of the pages left blank. There may not be a reason to say more because they said it all on the field during autumn Saturdays. They earned their reputations by their play, and they made their loyal followers proud.

This opening chapter of *Gopher Glory: The Pride of the Maroon and Gold* is a powerful proclamation specific to a person deeply connected to the future of Gopher football. Fans of the past, present and future have their hopes pinned to his leadership and direction. His name is Tim Brewster, and he is the head football coach of the Golden Gophers.

Brewster has a passion to win and honor the great tradition of Gopher football. He has a legacy to follow, and he is determined to uphold it while creating his own in the process. He wants to win, and he wants to reclaim success for all those faithful who have been waiting for decades.

Ask Brewster about Gopher tradition and he comes out of his office and emphatically points to the large mural in the hallway leading to his office. He looks directly at Hall of Famers Bobby Bell and Carl Eller and affirms their impact on the game of football.

The coach will talk about others on the mural, like Bud Grant and Bernie Bierman. And you will have no doubt about the coach's passion for Gopher tradition. You will have no doubt about the glory of the past and his confidence for the future. You will have no doubt that the Gophers will win again.

The tradition so resonates around Coach Brewster that after a conversation about Minnesota football with him, you desperately want to hear

the Gopher Rouser. You want go out and find someone to hit like the greats of the past did on those glorious Saturdays in the fall.

In positions of reverence on that mural outside Coach Brewster's office stand the pillars on which Minnesota football has been built: Bernie Bierman, Carl Eller, Bronko Nagurski, Bud Grant, Sandy Stephens, Tony Dungy, Bobby Bell and Coach Murray Warmath.

All left indelible marks on the Minnesota program and to this day remain beloved by the Gopher faithful.

This mural resides on the wall outside the office of Head Coach Tim Brewster.

***

The Bierman athletic complex where the great mural rests wasn't named by accident. Coach Bernie Bierman is a legend in Gopher football because of his great teams of the1930s and 40s. While leading the Golden Gophers, Bierman brought home five national championships, including three consecutive from 1934–1936.

When a college football coach and his team win a national championship, it solidifies greatness. It magnifies the heights of the profession. To win more than one, perhaps two, puts the coach among the elite. Bernie Bierman won five, including three in a row!

The mural features Bierman in coaching regalia, football type pants, no hat and a warm up jacket, pointing outwardly to the field. Coach Bierman must have seen something during practice that he didn't like and is calling attention to it. The look is stern but confident. There is a seriousness about his demeanor telling all that he is in charge. His pose conveys the look of a champion. He is Bernie Bierman, "the old Grey Eagle." Legendary figures don't come along very often in life. Legends earn their status and Bernie Bierman is a legend.

Next to Bierman, ready to charge the line, is the great Carl Eller. Number 76 played out his heroism for the maroon and gold, only to cement a further legacy with the Minnesota Vikings as one of the famed Purple People Eaters and a member of the National Football League Hall of Fame.

Eller brought football to new heights in devastating fashion. Former Minnesota Viking Jim Lindsey once said that Carl Eller had a physique that looked as if it had "been chiseled out of stone."

Looking at Eller in the mural, it is easy to see what Lindsey was talking about. His friends call him "Moose," a fitting description of his physicality and prowess on the gridiron. His athleticism was monster-like and he was one of the best that ever played the game, unstoppable on the field and true to the terms All-American and champion.

Next to Eller, looking as if to obliterate the opposition, stands the immortal Bronko Nagurski. Can you imagine a name like this representing anything else but football? It just wouldn't be right. Bronko Nagurski: the songwriter, poet, actor, violinist? Nothing against those honorable professions, but it doesn't fit. Bronko Nagurski: football player. A perfect match.

To most of those who had the honor of playing with him, Nagurski was one of the greatest football players ever. To many he symbolized the sheer force of the game during the 1930s. He was a Minnesota Gopher First Team All-American in 1929 at two positions, fullback and tackle, a feat no other college football player has ever duplicated. He enhanced his reputation for toughness with the Chicago Bears of the National Football League in the 1930s.

Nagurski was not known on the gridiron as a fancy or speedy runner. There wasn't much flash or spring to his running style. He didn't shock the crowds with his elusiveness while carrying the football. Nagurski just simply ran over the opposition. He was known as a straight-ahead power runner who used blunt force to demolish those who stood in his way. But Bronko Nagurski was not just a great runner; he was a brutal force when it came to blocking and tackling. He played four positions for the Gophers and was second to no one when it came to his defensive prowess later on for the Chicago Bears.

Nagurski's likeness features the old leather helmet without a facemask, allowing the onlooker to see his expression of power, pride and confidence. Nagurski's sheer strength and incredible feats on the field made him something special for Gopher fans to remember.

Next in line is Bud Grant. And as Grant follows the immortal three moving left to right across the mural, you notice they all are hovering over the old Memorial Stadium as it rests in the background, once home to the famous grouping of Gopher greats.

Perhaps the most recognized name in Minnesota sports history, Grant is depicted on the giant mural wearing Gopher gear and holding a football. Bud looks young, as he did when he played for the maroon and gold. Praised as one of the greatest athletes to step on to the University of Minnesota campus, Grant made a name for himself as a football, basketball and baseball player. Later he went on to the National Basketball Association with the Minneapolis Lakers, the National Football League as a player with the Philadelphia Eagles, the Canadian Football League as a player and championship coach with the Winnipeg Blue Bombers, and of course as the championship coach of the Minnesota Vikings. Bud Grant is a part of the legacy of Minnesota football and is rightfully placed on the great wall next to the others.

Next to Grant, flying high, feet in the air, ball in hand and about to hurdle an opponent for the goal line, is the renowned quarterback of the national championship 1960 Gophers and the Rose Bowl teams of 1961 and 1962, Sandy Stephens. He was a great athlete and a team leader recognized by fans, teammates and the opposition as one of the best to put on a Gopher uniform. Stephens' jersey is retired now and memories of his feats will live on. His achievements on the field solidify him as a major part of Gopher history.

A little below and to the right of Stephens is Gopher quarterback Tony Dungy. Dungy's leadership, character, commitment to a higher cause in life and championship years of coaching in the National Football League place him in a proper place on the great mural. Coach Brewster's recognition and appreciation for Tony Dungy is something special, and he is utilizing his legacy as a motivational tool for his own coaching and personal goals.

To the right of Dungy and slightly above him stands Bobby Bell. Bell, two-time All-American, Outland Trophy winner and a member of both the college and professional football Hall of Fame, is positioned as if he is coming right at you. You can try to block him, but you will likely fail as most did during his unparalleled college and professional career. Bobby Bell; enough said.

Standing at the end, jacket on with the collar rolled up, his "M" hat in place with the astute look of a football coach, is Murray Warmath. For eighteen seasons, Warmath strolled the sidelines of Memorial Stadium and the practice terrain of Northrop Field. He was the coach and everyone knew it.

Coach Brewster calls the Gopher comeback from the 1959 season to the national championship in 1960 the greatest story in the history of college football. Murray Warmath was the engineer and leader of it all. He was the boss. He took his Golden Gopher squad from a last place finish in the Big Ten Conference in 1959, to the national championship and the Rose Bowl following the 1960 season, a feat never achieved before or since.

If you look at the picture and see Warmath looking back, it won't take long for you to come to the conclusion that this man is a football coach. He looks the part, and his passion for the game is sacred to all who played for him. It wasn't possible for him to do anything else. Murray Warmath was born to coach football and he loved every minute of it.

And today, well into his 90s, he still is the penultimate coach.

The mural is right outside of Coach Brewster's office, commissioned by the coach himself. He knew about the past and he knew about the greatness of each who represents the hallowed University. Brewster knew the impact of those in the mural, and he wanted every player, coach, recruit, alum and visitor to see it as he or she walks near Brewster's office. He knew, and he wanted the mural to serve as a reminder every single day of the tradition of excellence the University of Minnesota program possesses.

Brewster plans to return the glory to Minnesota football, and as he so passionately states, "to reclaim what is rightfully ours! The national championship was ours in 1934, 1935 and 1936. And it was ours again in 1940, 1941 and 1960. And it will be ours again."

Seeing the passion coming from Coach Brewster, one would be foolish to try to convince the coach that there was a better player than Bobby Bell or Carl Eller. Or to try to name a better all around athlete than Bud Grant or find a list of coaches that won five national championships as Bernie Bierman did.

Tradition of the maroon and gold is more than just winning football games. It is more than dressing up on a Saturday afternoon to show your skills on the gridiron in front of thousands of people.

This tradition encompasses great players who have built a legacy of incredible athleticism, but are truly enshrined for the type of people they are and for what they represent.

A perfect example, and one of the greatest running backs to ever wear a Gopher uniform, was Number 44, Bob McNamara. His feats on the gridiron are legendary.

From 1952-54, McNamara brought crowds to their feet too often to count, for there were so many memorable runs and touchdowns. In 1954, McNamara won the Bronko Nagurski award as the Gophers' most valuable player, was selected All-Big Ten Conference, and was named an All-American. But McNamara's greatness is defined by the type of person he is and how he has maintained his passion for the University of Minnesota.

He was a senior player when Murray Warmath arrived for his first year to coach the Gophers.

"He was a great athlete," says Warmath. "He had speed, size and the

right kind of attitude. He stood head and shoulders above most and he
was a man when I arrived, and a bigger and better man as he got older,"
says Warmath proudly.

"He could do it all. He lives his life as a man, a great person and is one
of the best I have ever known."

And when it comes to a passion for winning, Coach Brewster will look
you straight in the eye and say, "No one wants the Gophers to win more
than Bob McNamara!"

So there was Bob McNamara, Nagurski and Grant, Bell and Eller, and
75 other first team All-Americans who wore the maroon and gold. Great
players of the past like Leo Nomellini, Clayton Tonnemaker, Francis
"Pug" Lund and a host of others that filled their role as the very best at
their positions and who built the tradition of Minnesota Golden Gopher
football.

Twenty Gopher greats were elected to the College Football Hall of
Fame and six former Gophers entered the Pro Football Hall of Fame.
As former Green Bay Packer Ray Nitschke once said about entering the
Hall, "You cannot be cut, traded, or waived from this football team. You
are a lifetime member."

And the maroon and gold is well-represented in that membership.

THE RIVALRIES

Gopher tradition is deep in winning records, championship seasons, honored players and hallowed symbols, symbols that recognized wins in the greatest of football rivalries. The Little Brown Jug, Floyd of Rosedale, Paul Bunyan's Axe and the Governor's Victory Bell all are symbolic of winning the big game against a fierce rival.

Likely the most famous of all football trophies has the label "The Little Brown Jug." Some would argue that the rivalry of the past several decades between Michigan and Ohio State may be greater; however, there is certainly no doubt that to the winner the "Jug" trophy is unmatched. And the story behind the "Little Brown Jug" makes it rich in Gopher lore.

It all started on October 31, 1903, when an underdog yet powerful Gopher football team battled to a 6-6 tie game against mighty Michigan before 20,000 frenzied fans at Northrop Field. The records show that the Gophers had averaged three to four thousand fans at most games that year, but the Michigan game drew almost seven times that number.

Michigan had rolled to 28 straight victories heading into Minneapolis. When the Gophers scored late in the game for the tie score, the game was prematurely halted as the fans poured on to the field.

Above: Gopher players with the Jug after a win at Michigan.

Left: Gopher players and fans celebrate capturing the Little Brown Jug after a victory over Michigan in 1960.

The day after the historic tie, a Gopher custodian found an old water jug near the Michigan side of the field and carried it to the athletic offices. He announced that the Michigan team had left their jug. When Fielding Yost, Michigan head football coach, sent a letter asking for the jug, he received a reply indicating that he would have to win the jug back, initiating one of the great rivalries in college football.

On November 15, 1924, Memorial Stadium was dedicated at the Illinois/Minnesota football game. In the dedication program under the heading "Some Highlights of the Past" appeared an article from George Barton, Sports Editor of the *Minneapolis Tribune*. It read in part:

"I believe the tensest moment I ever experienced while covering football games during the twenty-one years that I have written sports occurred as I watched Ed Rogers prepare to kick goal following the touchdown in that memorable struggle between Minnesota and Michigan at Northrop Field on the afternoon of October 31, 1903.

Forty-eight thousand eyes belonging to twenty-four thousand rabid football bugs were glued upon Minnesota's doughty captain and end, as he made ready for that try at goal which meant so much to the Gopher team and its followers. A heart-breaking defeat or a tie in the greatest game ever played upon a western gridiron, depended upon Rogers' trusty toe that afternoon. Imagine the situation. The two great teams had battled all afternoon and the players were in a state of exhaustion. Defeat had stared Minnesota in the face until the final minutes of play when the Gophers, by a superhuman effort, had rushed the ball down the field and across Michigan's goal line, leaving the score 6-5, in favor of the Wolverines. One point stood between Minnesota and a tie or defeat. It was up to Rogers to make that all-important point. Darkness had settled down over the field and it was with difficulty that spectators could make out the forms of the players. With the stoicism and deliberateness characteristic of the Indian, Rogers carefully measured the distance between the ball held by a teammate and the goal uprights. Then, three short, swift steps and thunk went Rogers' cleated shoe against the ball and it sailed squarely between the uprights for the point that the Minnesota players and adherents had prayed for. The crowd rushed upon the field and it was impossible for the policeman and officials to clear the gridiron. Because of the darkness and the fact that less than sixty seconds remained to be played, Captains Rogers and Redding agreed to call the game."

***

Floyd of Rosedale

Floyd of Rosedale is another of the coveted trophies in Gopher rivalry history. The old joke about southern state rival, Iowa, goes something like this: Do you know the greatest thing that ever happened to the state of Iowa? The answer: Interstate 35E North!

It seems over all, Minnesota and Iowa get along pretty well, except on Saturdays in the fall, when the Gophers head for Iowa City, or when the black and gold visit Minneapolis. For on these days, the Big Ten Conference and thousands of fans usually see a rugged, hard-nosed football game between the Gophers and the Hawkeyes. When the Gophers and Hawkeyes battle, they are playing for the right to keep the bronze statue of a pig called Floyd of Rosedale. The esteem of taking or keeping the pig has been something special since 1935.

The symbol of the great rivalry now takes the shape of a 15½-inch high, 21 inch long bronze statue of a prize hog, with quite a story behind its legendary status.

In 1935, the Gophers were in the middle of their national championship seasons and headed into Iowa for a huge game against their border rivals. The year before Minnesota had won a hard-fought and highly-contested battle, and many Iowa fans thought the Gophers had roughed up Iowa's star player, Ozzie Simmons. The furor over the game was so intense that Iowa's governor, Clyde Herring, publicly proclaimed, "If the officials stand for any rough tactics like Minnesota used last year, I'm sure the crowd won't."

Minnesota governor Floyd Olson, in an attempt to cool the temperatures that were rising as the game got closer, sent off a message to his Iowa counterpart and proclaimed his confidence in Iowa fans remaining "law abiding," and further stated to the Iowa governor, "I will bet you a Minnesota prize hog against an Iowa prize hog that Minnesota wins."

Governor Olsen's gesture did ease the tension for the game, and the Gophers came out on top by a score of 13-6.

The Gophers returned home with the win and a prize Iowa hog named "Floyd of Rosedale," named after the Governor of Minnesota and the farm it came from, Rosedale Farms near Fort Dodge, Iowa. The hog was delivered by Iowa Governor Herring, who personally walked Floyd into Governor Olsen's office. The hog was later won by a student in an essay-writing contest and sold to the University of Minnesota. The university subsequently sold the prize hog to a hog breeder located near the Minnesota-Iowa border.

After Floyd's death, Governor Olsen commissioned the bronze sculpture as a symbol of good sportsmanship and the great rivalry between Minnesota and Iowa, and each university takes on the challenge to house Floyd of Rosedale in their trophy case, representing a win in their seasonal battles.

Another border battle has brought great tradition to the longest series of games played in college football Division1-A history. Minnesota and Wisconsin have played 117 games and counting. Records have to be traced back to 1890 for the start of this great rivalry, with the Gophers winning the first game 63-0.

The Gophers and Badgers play every year for the coveted trophy known as "Paul Bunyan's Axe." The winning team in 1930 was awarded a fashionable "Slab of Bacon," made out of black walnut created by Dr. R.B. Fouch, symbolic of "bringing home the bacon" for the win. It was an attempt to create a trophy comparable to the Little Brown Jug.

It took many years and many embroiled battles for the Axe to take its place in Gopher-Badger history. But as more ceremonies transferring the Slab of Bacon to the winner were cancelled due to often disruptive behavior by

Gopher players with the Paul Bunyan Axe.

fans, the award fell out of favor. In fact, the Slab of Bacon trophy disappeared only to be recovered in an old Wisconsin storage room some five decades later. But the scores were recorded on the old trophy and have been transferred to the Axe, and one of the great rivalries in college football carries on.

***

A final rivalry comes fairly recently to Gopher football. The game between the Gophers and Penn State earns the winner the coveted Governor's Victory Bell trophy. It started on September 4, 1993. Like Floyd of Rosedale, this tradition began by a couple of state governors flexing their muscles in pride for their home universities.

The Bell signifies the first Big Ten football game for Penn State after its admission to the conference, and for Minnesota a welcoming in as the first opponent for the newest conference member. By the addition of the Governor's Victory Bell Trophy to the Gopher schedule, Minnesota now has four active "trophy games" on its schedule, more than any other college football team in the country.

So, if it is tradition you want, it is all here with Minnesota Golden Gopher football. But tradition comes in many forms. And it often comes rushing back to the forefront in the form

The Governor's Victory Bell

of wonderful memories from the past.

***

When it comes to passion for Minnesota Gopher football, it is hard to find anyone more passionate than Steve Neils. When former Gopher Neils starts talking maroon and gold football, there is little doubt that he is close to climbing back into uniform and carrying on the intensity and excitement that remains within him since starring for Minnesota in 1971-73, earning First Team All Big Ten honors his senior year.

But Steve Neils was not just another college scholarship football player on a Division 1-A football team. Steve listened intently to every Gopher game on the radio and attended several during his early years.

Steve Neils

"I remember exactly where I was when the Gophers lost the disastrous nightmare battle on Wisconsin's turf in 1962," recalls Steve. "All I ever wanted to do growing up was to play football for the Gophers."

Do you want tradition, great memories, unforgettable highlights? Well, just ask Steve Neils. He is likely to mention the greatest pre-game talk he ever heard given by a football coach.

"Cal Stoll gave the speech before the Michigan game in 1972," says Steve. "And I will never forget it because it brought the team together."

That speech before the Michigan game has had such an impact on Steve that he is convinced it created a bond for the Gophers that year. To hear Steve recall the Stoll talk, you might think he heard it yesterday, not some 36 years ago.

The Gophers traveled to Ann Arbor in 1972, a beaten down squad after losing its first five of six games. An earlier victory over Iowa gave some hope to the maroon and gold that afternoon, but before the opening kick off, the 84,000 Michigan fans and the Michigan Marching Band had dimmed the glimmer of hope, as the highly-ranked Wolverines prepared for the 1-5 Gophers.

It didn't help that the Gopher locker room was

Former Golden Gopher Head Coach Cal Stoll

being bombarded by the Michigan band playing right outside the locker room before the game. Perhaps this was all strategy on the part of the Michigan faithful to further demoralize the Gophers.

As the noise of the Michigan band ripped through the doors of the Gopher locker room, Coach Cal Stoll entered.

"I know exactly how you feel at this moment," said Stoll, "because I feel the same way. Last night when I tried to go to sleep and realized it was for naught, I followed a routine that I have when I can't sleep. I picked up a history book."

As the Gopher players listened intently, Stoll told of reading about Leonidas, the King of Sparta, a Greek general known for his strength and bravery. He described how this great warrior took his men of 300 strong into the Battle of Thermopylae to defend against a Persian invasion.

It was 480 BC and Leonidas had set out to meet Xerxes' army in an incredibly overmatched position. Although Leonidas had slightly more than 300 fighters, he was outnumbered by some estimates of hundreds of thousands. And when a message to surrender reached him, he said to his men, "We will fight in the shade."

Surrendering rather than fighting to the end was simply not an option.

With this thought in mind, Stoll looked at his underdog squad and said, "Men, let's go fight in the shade."

Neils recalls the locker room exploded like nothing he had ever witnessed. The Gophers roared out on to the field right through the Wolverine band and onto the storied Michigan gridiron, their "Battle of Thermopylae."

Steve Neils did all he could do to keep under control. He was on the kick-off team and was convinced that he would hit the ball carrier and cause an immediate fumble. After all, this was really Leonidas and the Battle of Thermopylae taking place, not just a football game between Minnesota and Michigan.

And when it was over, there was devastation. The game ended in resounding fashion. Final score: Michigan 42 Minnesota 0.

That was not a misprint. The teams aren't inverted on the page. It ended Michigan 42 and Minnesota 0. How could this be?

What about the great pre-game pep talk from Cal Stoll? What about Leonidas and the Battle of Themopylae? Did the Gophers go out that afternoon at Ann Arbor and change the course of Greek history?

Maybe they did, or maybe Cal Stoll knew exactly what he was doing.

The next day the Gophers filed into their meeting room to go over the game films of the disaster at Ann Arbor. To a man, they were convinced that Coach Stoll was going to go berserk, chewing them out like never before. They had let him down, the team down, and most of all the University. They were convinced this film session was going to get ugly.

As the Gopher players sat with their heads down in despair, Stoll entered the room and quietly and calmly addressed the team.

"Men, I know exactly how you feel. I feel the same way you do. Last night when I couldn't sleep, I pulled out my history book and began reading it as I always do. And I finished reading about Leonidas and the

Battle of Thermopylae."

The team, feeling greater despair as they thought about the victorious reign of the legendary Leonidas, was shocked at what they heard.

"Leonidas was completely wiped out," proclaimed Stoll. "He never had a chance."

There was silence.

Stoll didn't have to say another word. The players' heads came up and a bond formed that Steve Neils recalls set the tone for great games ahead.

The following week, the Gophers barely lost to a highly-ranked Ohio State team, and then went on to win the rest of their games, beating Northwestern, Michigan State and Wisconsin. They had become a team that day in the film room, and Cal Stoll was their leader.

Leonidas would have been proud!

Stoll knew exactly what he was doing. He understood college football players and he had a unique ability to say things at the right time, delivering words of wisdom that had great meaning.

Neils recalls another of Coach Stoll's comments that has always remained with him: "60 minutes to play and a lifetime to remember."

For Steve Neils, playing for the Gophers was truly a dream come true. He went on to have a fine career in the National Football League with the St. Louis Cardinals. But what mattered the most for Neils is that he really did fulfill his childhood dream. He played football for the Golden Gophers.

One of the things that has bothered Neils greatly through the years is when a Minnesota high school football talent chooses to go to another state to play college football.

"It absolutely kills me when kids go other places to play," says Neils.

Neils was not offered a scholarship to play for the Gophers when he graduated from St. Peter High School. He decided to go to Deerfield Academy, an eastern prep school. After one year at Deerfield, his prowess on the field had earned him the opportunity to play football at the college level. His football coach came to him at the end of the season and advised him that he had earned the right to go to any school of his choosing.

"Where do you want to go?" asked Coach Smith, "Michigan, Ohio State, USC?"

"I want to go to Minnesota," said Neils.

"No really, where do you want to go?" said the coach.

Again, the only answer was, "Minnesota."

Neils knew if he went to Michigan or Ohio State, he would end up being another face from another place, but Minnesota was a place to continue to call home, a place where a local player can make a difference on and off the field.

Now in the business world, Neils' love for Golden Gopher football remains.

"If I could just step out of this suit and go out and hit someone again it would be wonderful," says Neils, with a gleam in his eye. "I always gave everything I had," he recalls. "I never wanted to let end coach Butch Nash down. I was so proud to have been one of Butch's boys. He was such a great coach and he loved Golden Gopher football more than anyone. It was an honor to play for him."

***

So many former players have kept alive their passion for Gopher football and truly represent the traditions of the maroon and gold.

Keith Simons played for the Gophers from 1972-1975 and had the esteemed honor of being named captain of the team in 1975.

"I loved playing for the Gophers," says Simons, "and I really enjoyed Cal Stoll. He had tremendous credibility with the players and me, and is one of the main reasons that I came to Minnesota. I learned to practice hard and play hard, and having a great work ethic and preparing well was very important to me, and to lead others in this regard."

Simons is one of the former players that can't wait to get back on campus with Gopher football.

"It will be unbelievable, the marching band, the sounds, it is going to be great again," says Simons.

***

Greg Engebos played for the Gophers from 1972-1974 and was an outstanding player. Engebos also liked playing for Stoll.

"I want the opportunity to be able to give back to a tremendous football program," says Engebos. "I always enjoyed playing for Coach Stoll, but I also thought that Murray Warmath had been a great coach at

Minnesota for all those years that he was there. Cal Stoll was a great human being, had a tremendous character and was somewhat of a historian. I loved playing for the Gophers. You found special connections with the players, coaches, the University of Minnesota and the city. It was all special and still is," says Engebos.

"I remember being in Coach Warmath's office and saying something to the effect of not being sure I can do this and live up to the expectations that they had for me. Coach Warmath leaned over his desk and said to me, 'If I didn't think you could play, you would not be here!' I will never forget it."

***

Bruce Suneson wore the maroon and gold from 1964-1966.

"My grandparents lived near the stadium, and we used to be over there often on Saturdays listening to the Gopher games on the radio," said Suneson. "And we were close enough so we could hear the roar from the crowd, and it was unbelievable!

"When I was growing up, I was like most other kids, dreaming of some day playing for the Gophers. Once I got into the program, it really molded my future for me. I learned about never giving up, and the experience helped shape my beliefs in life. I had the opportunity to get to know many great players and wonderful people who were also Golden Gophers," recalls Suneson. "For me, it was truly an honor to wear the colors. And being around Coach Warmath was really amazing. He was bigger than life to me, and he had such a great memory. He never forgot anything and he knew so much about football."

***

A great linebacker for the Gophers was Gary Reierson, who played from 1964-1966, and once recorded 17 tackles in a game. Reierson was a hard-hitting defender who always around the ball. Reierson often speaks of the great pride he had while wearing the maroon and gold. He was a great athlete who also played baseball for the Gophers. Look around at events involving Gopher football and Gary Reierson will be there, with the same passion he had when he ran onto the field on Saturday afternoons.

***

From another time and a different era is Sean Hoffman, a great player for the Gophers from 1997-2000. He was a holdover from the Coach Jim Wacker era into the Glen Mason coaching years. Hoffman enjoyed both coaches and found great qualities in each.

"Coach Wacker was such a good person and really loved his players," says Hoffman. "But I liked playing for Glen Mason, too. If you did your job and did things the right way, he treated you very well," recalls Hoffman. "He was very even keeled and a good coach."

Hoffman says it's an honor to be a part of Gopher football, and he desperately wants the team to start to win again. He lives by the words, "We are one game from going from loser to winner and the football program needs to be in a better place than past history has accounted for."

"Mason taught us that every week. We had to earn our right to be a Big Ten football player and that has really stuck with me," says Hoffman. "It was a great lesson."

***

Deryl Ramey grew up loving Gopher football and fulfilled his dream to play for Minnesota, suiting up from 1963-1965 as a center, long snapper and kicker. Ramey was a freshman during the great 1962 Gopher season.

"It was everything to me to be able to play for the Gophers," says Ramey. "I always dreamed of that when I was growing up. When I came as a freshman, I got to go up against some of the greatest of all time. Players like Julian Hook, Bobby Bell, Tom Deegan, they were all still here from the great teams of the early 1960s. I was recruited to Minnesota as a quarterback and linebacker and they switched me to center. It took a while for me to get used to it, but I loved it. I also love what Coach Brewster is doing," says Ramey. "He has really made us feel connected to the program again."

***

Great passion and love for the Gophers also runs deep with Justin Conzemius who played for Minnesota from 1992-1995. He was a team captain in 1995 and an Academic All-American in 1994 and again in 1995.

"Playing for Minnesota was very special," says Conzemius. "The Big Ten is the premier conference in college football and the Minnesota rivalries are really something. I loved playing for Jim Wacker. He apologized to us after every loss. He was a great football coach and the players loved him. When I was named captain, Coach Wacker said to me, 'Be who you are, don't change, lead the team by example.'"

And Justin Conzemius has done just that since graduation. He is a professional in the business world and proudly carries the tradition of Golden Gopher football with him.

***

Gopher tradition extends over the past century from the early games on the old Northrop Field, to Memorial Stadium, the Metrodome, and the brand new on-campus TCF Bank Stadium, opening in the fall of 2009.

This chapter could go on forever with stories about the rich tradition of Golden Gopher football. So we end the traditions with the recognition of the Retired Numbers and Retired Jerseys, knowing that the future will provide more names to add to the list.

We honor those who are recognized by the fans and the University of Minnesota. There is no higher proclamation of thank you, no higher proclamation of fame.

NUMBER 72 Bronko Nagurski - was he the best to ever play the game? He might have been. Number retired October 27, 1979.

NUMBER 54 Bruce Smith - Heisman Trophy winner and great All-American. Number retired June 27, 1977.

NUMBER 10 Paul Giel - Great running back, runner up to the Heisman Trophy and two-time All-American. Number retired September 24, 1991.

NUMBER 15 Sandy Stephens - National Championship and Rose Bowl quarterback. Jersey retired November 18, 2000.

2

THE NATIONAL CHAMPIONS

Dave Mona, Minnesota Gophers' football radio analyst, has a perspective on the past relative to the number of years since the Gophers were champions. While a University of Minnesota student, Dave was a reporter for the *Minnesota Daily*, the student newspaper, and had an opportunity to go to the Gophers' Rose Bowl game in Pasadena, California, following the 1961 season.

It was the Gophers' second trip in two years to the "Grand Daddy of all Bowls." Dave could make the trip for $68, slightly less costly 46 years ago than today, however significant dollars to a student back then. Not having the money on hand, Dave thought, "I don't need to go this year. I can make the next one, since the Gophers seem to be going to the Rose Bowl on a regular basis."

It has been four and a half decades since that 1962 appearance, and Dave is still waiting.

The word champion is often used to describe being the best at something, and in the world of college football, "champions" are declared when a team wins a national championship. The Gophers reached this ultimate victory six times over the decades, more than most college football teams can ever dream of achieving. Only three other collegiate football programs have won more.

1934 NATIONAL CHAMPIONS

The 1934 champions were a great running team, attacking their opponents with four All-Americans on the squad. There are football teams that go decades without having a player earn All-American honors, but the 1934 Gopher football team featured Francis "Pug" Lund, Bill Bevan, Bob Tenner and Frank "Butch" Larson.

Lund was named an All-American in 1933 and 1934, and averaged almost six yards per carry in 1934, when he was also the team captain. He was a tremendous football player, accomplishing gridiron feats that led the Gopher squad to greatness.

Also an All-American on the national championship team of 1934 was Frank "Butch" Larson, who was devastating as a Gopher end. He was known for his incredible hard-hitting style of play and his brilliant punt coverage. Larson's great leadership and dominant play was a catalyst for the undefeated season.

In addition to Lund and Larson, the Gopher arsenal also included Bill Bevan, a powerful force at the guard position. Bevan was one of the last college football players to play without a helmet and was thought to be one of the toughest players of the 1930s era. Bevan not only demoralized opponents with his hard hitting, but also kicked extra points for the Gophers.

Bob Tenner was an outstanding end for the Gophers, a three year letterman and an All-American in 1934. He made some great plays for Minnesota, perhaps his best was his reception of a pass from "Pug" Lund for a touchdown to defeat Pittsburgh. The origin of the play started with a handoff to Glenn Seidel from Stan Kostka, a subsequent lateral to Lund and the pass to Tenner. In reflecting upon the past history of Gopher football, former head coach Bernie Bierman, has recalled this Tenner touchdown as one of his greatest memories.

The Gophers were coming off a 4-0-4 season in 1933 and knew the 1934 team had potential. The team opened the season with a crushing 56-12 win over North Dakota and followed with a 20-0 win over Nebraska.

In the third game of the season, it took two incredible plays from Butch Larson to ensure a Gopher win over the Pittsburgh Panthers. With the Gophers trailing most of the game, Larson recovered a fumble in the fourth quarter, which led to a touchdown, and then on the next series was successful with a touchdown pass for the 13-7 victory.

Next it was Iowa and a 48-12 Minnesota win, as the Gophers logged 514 yards in total offense to a meager 129 for the Hawkeyes. The following week Michigan came to Memorial Stadium and left after a 34-0 thrashing.

But it wasn't just the great play of Pug Lund, Larson and Bevan leading the Gophers. The Iowa game featured the running of Stan Kostka, who scored three touchdowns, and Julius Alfonse who scored twice. And in the Michigan game five different Gophers contributed to the scoring.

It proved to be a great defeat of Michigan that year, as the Gophers had not taken possession of the Little Brown Jug since 1927. The Wolverines were outplayed, managing only 56 total yards for the entire game.

In the Indiana game the following week, the Gophers held the Hoosiers to an unbelievable zero total yards, and the next week against Chicago the total yards gained by the opponents was just 82.

In the games against Michigan, Indiana and Chicago, the 1934 Gopher defense gave up a total of just 138 yards.

The Gopher squad amassed outstanding statistics from both sides of the line. On offense the Gophers averaged 325 yards per game while the defense held its opponents to a weak 4.7 points and 103 yard average per game. It was a remarkable season and the first national championship for the Minnesota Gophers.

1934 SEASON RECORD 8-0-0
BIG TEN CONFERENCE RECORD 5-0-0

September 29	Minnesota 56	North Dakota State 0	
October 6	Minnesota 20	Nebraska 0	
October 20	Minnesota 13	Pittsburgh 7	(at Pittsburgh)
October 27	Minnesota 48	Iowa 12	(at Iowa)
November 3	Minnesota 34	Michigan 0	
November 10	Minnesota 30	Indiana 0	
November 17	Minnesota 35	Chicago 7	
November 24	Minnesota 34	Wisconsin 0	(at Wisconsin)

The 1934 national champions had the aforementioned four All-Americans on the roster as well as six All-Big Ten players in Bevan, Larson, Lund, Tenner, and tackles Phil Bengsten and Ed Widseth.

Widseth and Lund were later inducted into the College Football Hall of Fame as well.

1935 NATIONAL CHAMPIONS

Coach Bernie Bierman's 1935 team was faced with the graduation of the 1934 squad's four All-Americans. Most teams would find rebounding to another title difficult under those conditions, unless the unusual situation of having four more All-Americans surface in the following season occurs.

In 1935, it did.

Four more Gophers played their way to this famed status and led the 1935 Gophers to a second national championship by going undefeated for a second consecutive season. It was a wonderful season for Minnesota football, and it included a victory over Iowa in the memorable game where Floyd of Rosedale was first introduced, paving the way to what would become a hard-fought rivalry.

The 1935 season was Coach Bernie Bierman's fourth at the helm, and despite the loss of Lund, Larson, Tenner and Bevan, there were very high hopes for future All-Americans Ed Widseth and Dick Smith at the tackle positions, Bud Wilkinson at guard and Sheldon Biese at the fullback spot. Quarterback Babe LaVoir also played a key role on the dominating 1935 squad.

The 1935 schedule was similar to the previous year's, with the Gophers taking on North Dakota State and Nebraska in the first two games. Although the Minnesota team was victorious in both games, the wins weren't as dominating as in the previous season. Defeating the Cornhuskers 20-0 in 1934, the Gophers barely squeaked out a 12-7 win at Lincoln in 1935.

The 1935 team was a different type of squad, and although the offense was not putting up the big scores, the defense was again extraordinary. Nebraska was able to gain only five first downs in the entire game, and the following week Tulane gained only 60 yards at Memorial Stadium. The next week against the Northwestern Wildcats, it took a great interception from Bud Wilkinson to place the Gophers in to the victory column, with a final score of 21-13.

Because the team lacked the incredible offensive punch of the previous campaign, there was some concern about the upcoming schedule. However, the Gophers went on to destroy the rest of the competition, by the cumulative score of 115-20. The offense began to click and the defense became even more dominant, as the Gophers rolled over everyone in their path.

All-American Sheldon Biese led the way for the Gophers in the last four contests, scoring seven touchdowns while running the ball practically at will. The only true test for the Gophers came against the Iowa Hawkeyes at Iowa City. In the end, the Gophers prevailed, besting Iowa 13-7. The team enjoyed its 40-0 whipping of bitter rival Michigan at Ann Arbor, then went on to defeat the Badgers to wrap up another 8-0-0 season and a second consecutive national championship.

1935 SEASON RECORD 8-0-0
BIG TEN CONFERENCE RECORD 5-0-0

September 28	Minnesota 26	North Dakota State 6	
October 12	Minnesota 12	Nebraska 7	(at Nebraska)
October 19	Minnesota 20	Tulane 0	
October 26	Minnesota 21	Northwestern 13	
November 2	Minnesota 29	Purdue 7	
November 9	Minnesota 13	Iowa 6	(at Iowa)
November 16	Minnesota 40	Michigan 0	(at Michigan)
November 23	Minnesota 33	Wisconsin 7	

The 1935 national championship team included four All-Americans: halfback Sheldon Biese, tackle Dick Smith, tackle Ed Widseth and guard Charles "Bud" Wilkinson. Five Gophers made the All-Big Ten team in 1935: Biese, Smith, Widseth, Wilkinson, and quarterback Vernal "Babe" LaVoir. Ed Widseth was later elected to the College Football Hall of Fame.

1936 NATIONAL CHAMPIONS

Going into the 1936 season, the Gophers had accumulated 17 straight victories, so expectations remained high for a third national championship. However, a much tougher schedule of non-conference opponents faced the Gophers. The team faced the University of Washington and Texas as opponents instead of North Dakota State and Tulane.

The opening game in Seattle almost didn't occur.

On the way out to the game, the Gophers had to evacuate their hotel in an early morning hour due to a fire, but managed to escape safely, travel to the coast and defeat the Huskies 14-7 before a packed stadium crowd cheering on their University of Washington team.

The Gophers were led to victory by the running of Julian Alphonse and the amazing play of Bud Wilkinson, who knocked down several passes, kicked two points after touchdowns and caught a 60 yard pass to put the Gophers in scoring position late in the game. Alphonse's running game was spectacular, and he knocked down three passes at the goal line to prevent Washington from a late-game score.

After the long trip to the coast and back by train, the Gophers were barely able to defeat Nebraska the following week, but the defense held strong in the 7-0 win.

The next two games really proved the Gophers' worth as they soundly defeated Michigan 26-0 and Purdue 33-0. The Michigan win, the third consecutive over the Wolverines, made the national championship seasons even sweeter. The Gophers had defeated Michigan by scores of 34-0, 40-0, and 26-0. It would be 1943 before the Wolverines would finally defeat the Gophers and recapture the Little Brown Jug.

The 1936 Minnesota team was on a roll and looking for a third straight undefeated season, as they entered Evanston to play the Northwestern Wildcats. However, dreadful weather conditions prohibited either team from creating any formidable offense, and the game moved into the fourth quarter scoreless.

Finally, Northwestern scored but missed the conversion kick and lead 6-0. The Gophers put together three drives in the final quarter, but were unable to break into the scoring column and fell to defeat. It was the first loss for the maroon and gold in 28 games and ended the possibility of yet another undefeated season.

As the season continued, the Gophers rallied for resounding wins against their remaining opponents. And then something amazing occurred. Even though the Gophers suffered the loss to Northwestern and failed to defend their Big Ten title, they were once again voted national champions. Their total dominance during the 1936 season, allowing only three teams to score all year, was enough to earn them a third consecutive national championship.

1936 SEASON RECORD 7-1-0
BIG TEN CONFERENCE RECORD 4-1-0

September 26	Minnesota 14	Washington 7	(at Washington)
October 10	Minnesota 7	Nebraska 0	
October 17	Minnesota 26	Michigan 0	

October 24	Minnesota 33	Purdue 0	
October 31	Minnesota 0	Northwestern 6	(at Northwestern)
November 7	Minnesota 52	Iowa 0	
November 14	Minnesota 47	Texas 19	
November 21	Minnesota 24	Wisconsin 0	(at Wisconsin)

The 1936 national champions featured All-American tackle and future College Hall of Famer Ed Widseth. The Gophers also had two All-Big Ten players in Widseth and halfback Andy Uram.

Losses to Nebraska and Notre Dame in 1937 ended the coveted title streak, and six total losses the following two seasons kept the Gophers from national recognition during the 1937-39 seasons. And then the 1940 season arrived, and Bierman showed the country that the University of Minnesota had returned to national prominence.

1940 NATIONAL CHAMPIONSHIP

After the national championship run from 1934-1936, the Gophers suffered their first losing season under head football coach Bernie Bierman in 1939, going 3-4-1. After the accomplishments of the previous years the losing record was tough on the team and the Gopher faithful.

But it was soon to be forgotten as the 1940 season began with wins over Washington and Nebraska. The Gophers were underdogs in both games but overcame the odds to notch victories.

After studying the Minnesota-Washington game, the Cornhuskers were determined to shut down the running attack of George Franck and Bruce Smith, but didn't know the Gophers were going to throw Bill Dailey and William Johnson at them. The pair gained close to 300 yards, solidifying the win for Minnesota.

Three more wins followed, over Ohio State, Iowa and Northwestern. Running backs Franck and Smith, both First Team All-Americans (Franck in 1940 and Smith in 1941), led the Gophers. Franck scored four touchdowns in the Iowa game, leading the Gophers to a dominating 34-6 victory.

The Northwestern game was thought to be a tough match and it proved to be so with Minnesota squeaking out a 13-12 win. The games between the two had always been close. From 1932-1949, no game between Minnesota and Northwestern was decided by more than one touchdown.

Michigan was next and the score was equally close, with the Gophers prevailing 7-6. Bruce Smith was the star of the game, rushing for 116 yards, including an 80-yard touchdown run to seal the victory.

Bruce Smith's father, Lucius Smith, was in the stands that day to watch his son score the game-winning touchdown. It must have been very satisfying to the former Gopher, who blamed himself for a loss to Michigan three decades earlier. With decisive wins over Purdue and Wisconsin, the Gophers wrapped up another perfect season and claimed their fourth national championship.

1940 SEASON RECORD 8-0-0
BIG TEN CONFERENCE RECORD 6-0-0

September 28	Minnesota 19	Washington 14	
October 5	Minnesota 13	Nebraska 7	
October 19	Minnesota 13	Ohio State 7	(at Ohio State)
October 26	Minnesota 34	Iowa 6	
November 2	Minnesota 13	Northwestern 12	(at Northwestern)
November 9	Minnesota 7	Michigan 6	
November 16	Minnesota 33	Purdue 0	
November 23	Minnesota 22	Wisconsin 13	(at Wisconsin)

The 1940 national champions had two All-Americans on the team: halfback George Franck and tackle Urban Odson. George Franck later went on to be elected to the College Football Hall of Fame. Both Franck and Odson were All-Big Ten players as well.

The 1940 national championship season avenged the 1937, 1938 and 1939 title-less seasons. The remarkable string of three national championships and a combined record over the 1934-36 seasons of 23 wins and one loss not only established one of the greatest championship runs in college football history, but previewed what was to come as the 1940's began.

The Gophers were on top again and there were high hopes for the 1941 season as the squad, University and loyal fans looked toward a fifth national championship season. And it soon arrived.

1941 NATIONAL CHAMPIONSHIP

The Gophers winning another national championship was almost too much to ask.

Coach Bernie Bierman had already won four of them and had four undefeated seasons on his resume. But the 1941 Gopher team was a team of champions. Led by Heisman Trophy winner Bruce Smith and All-American tackle Dick Wildung, the Gophers were not to be stopped. They had a tough Big Ten conference schedule as well as games against national powers Washington and Nebraska again, so another championship would be challenging.

Although Bruce Smith captured the coveted Heisman Trophy, he proved to be only the third leading rusher for Minnesota that season. However, Smith excelled in so many other ways on the field that he truly was the team leader and contributed significantly to the undefeated season.

Washington was a tough opponent with which to open the season, and it took monumental efforts from Bill Dailey and Bruce Smith to lead the Gophers to a hard-fought 14-6 win in Seattle.

The Gophers found that Illinois and Pittsburgh provided little competition as the season continued, and a 7-0 win over Michigan the following week kept the Gophers undefeated.

In the Northwestern game, Bruce Smith was injured and Bud Higgins stepped up and rushed for 96 yards, leading the team to victory.

With Iowa on the road and Smith still injured, the Gopher season was on the line. Smith, however, convinced Coach Bierman to let him play in the game. He set up three Gopher scores and an ultimate 34-13 win at Iowa City.

A 41-6 victory over the Wisconsin Badgers sealed another perfect season and a fifth national championship for the Golden Gophers. With this season-ending victory, Bernie Bierman became the winningest coach in Gopher football history.

The 1941 season ended the reign of Bierman's national championship seasons from 1934-1936 and 1940-1941.

1941 SEASON RECORD 8-0-0
BIG TEN CONFERENCE RECORD 5-0-0

September 27	Minnesota 14	Washington 6	(at Washington)
October 11	Minnesota 34	Illinois 6	
October 18	Minnesota 39	Pittsburgh 0	
October 25	Minnesota 7	Michigan 0	(at Michigan)
November 1	Minnesota 8	Northwestern 7	
November 8	Minnesota 9	Nebraska 0	
November 15	Minnesota 34	Iowa 13	(at Iowa)
November 22	Minnesota 41	Wisconsin 6	

The 1941 national champions had two All-Americans: halfback Bruce Smith and tackle Dick Wildung. Smith went on to win the Heisman Trophy that year and was later elected to the College Football Hall of Fame. He was an All-Big Ten player along with Wildung, halfback Bill Daily, end Bob Fitch, and guard Len Levy.

In 1942, with Bernie Bierman gone on military status, Dr. George Hauser coached the Gophers and their record fell to 5-4-1 and 3-3-0 in the Big Ten. A 50-0 win over Pittsburgh to begin the season gave great hope for another championship run, but losses to Iowa and Illinois quickly dimmed the hopes.

A 15-2 win at Nebraska and 16-14 win over Michigan kept the record respectable; however, losses to Indiana and Wisconsin closed out a tumultuous and ultimately disappointing season.

In 1943 Michigan was able to re-capture the Little Brown Jug after throttling the maroon and gold at Ann Arbor by a score of 49-6, and a 42-6 loss the following week at Northwestern set the tone for what was ahead.

The 1944 Gopher season was not much better, with losses to Iowa, Michigan and Ohio State. But a tie to Northwestern closed the season with a 5-3-1 record. Dr. George Hauser finished his three seasons at the Gopher helm with a 15-11-1 record, and the team anxiously anticipated the return of Bernie Bierman to begin the 1945 campaign.

Despite high hopes for the Gophers to return to the national spotlight under Coach Bierman, it was not to be. Bierman guided the Gophers to early wins against Missouri, Nebraska, Fort Warren and Northwestern. However, the Gophers lost the last five games of the season to Ohio State, Michigan, Indiana, Iowa and Wisconsin.

During the next five seasons, the Gophers were unable to reach the previous championship level. However, Bierman's teams did finish a very respectable 7-2 in 1948 and again in 1949, led by the great play of All-Americans Leo Nomellini and Clayton Tonnemaker.

Michigan continued to prove a tough foe for the Gophers as the Wolverines won their seventh straight from Minnesota in 1949, 14-7.

In 1950, Bierman's final year as head coach, the Gophers finished a disappointing 1-7-1 and 1-4-1 in the Big Ten. After the first five games in 1950, a tie with Michigan was the best the team could accomplish, and the remaining games saw losses to Iowa, Michigan State and Wisconsin. Only a victory over Purdue kept the Gophers from a winless season.

For the next three years, Wes Fesler was the Gophers coach and his Gopher squads recorded only ten wins, but were inspired by the great play of All-Americans Paul Giel and Bob McNamara, two of the greatest running backs to ever wear the maroon and gold.

In 1954 Murray Warmath came to the Gophers and stayed as the head coach for the next 18 seasons. Warmath had the benefit of Bob McNamara in his backfield in 1954 and the Gophers secured a promising 7-2 season, with four wins to open the year.

From 1957 to 1959, however, the Gophers had a stretch of losing seasons that was difficult on all concerned. A 4-5 record was followed by 1-8 and 2-7 seasons, and Warmath faced a difficult challenge to turn things around.

During these very disappointing seasons in the late fifties, the Gophers were not among the elite of the Big Ten. Murray Warmath received some rough treatment after the 1958-1959 seasons, and his job was in turmoil, with little sense of the national prominence Minnesota would soon regain.

As the 1960 season began, no one knew what was ahead.

1960 NATIONAL CHAMPIONS

The 1960 season brought out some of the greatest players in Gopher football history. Names like Bobby Bell and Sandy Stephens and Tom Brown brought football back to the northland with legendary acclaim.

The Gophers started out with a 26-14 win over Nebraska, a surprise to many because the Gophers were given little chance to beat the Cornhuskers. Tom Brown and quarterback Sandy Stephens paved the way for the opening season win, as Stephens was proficient both passing and punting the football. The win was satisfying, but no one was getting on the bandwagon just yet. The previous two seasons had been too much of a disappointment.

Against Indiana in game two, the Gophers came alive in the fourth quarter and scored four touchdowns on the way to a 42-0 route, which started raising eyebrows about the potential of the 1960 team.

Northwestern was the next opponent, a tough test from a team that had beaten the Gophers the two previous seasons. Led by quarterback Dick Thornton, the Wildcats challenged Minnesota, but it was Tom Brown, the Gophers' outstanding lineman, who stole the show. Brown was devastating on defense, and at the end of the day Thornton's rushing statistics recorded a lowly minus 14 yards running the football.

Up next for Minnesota was a tough Illinois team at Memorial Stadium. The Gophers again prevailed, this time with a potent offense run by quarterback Sandy Stephens who accounted for all three Gopher touchdowns in a 21-10 win.

The Gophers next defeated Michigan, Kansas State and a great Iowa team that came into Memorial Stadium ranked as the top team in the nation. Suddenly the Minnesota Gophers found themselves 7-0, leading the Big Ten and ranked first in the polls.

The win streak ended the next week in a shocking loss to a weak Purdue squad, but the Gophers didn't let the defeat upset their season, as they prevailed in an impressive 26-7 win over Wisconsin at Madison to end the 1960 season.

The Gophers finished number one in the polls and claimed the national championship for the sixth time. In addition, the Gophers earned their first trip to Pasadena and the Rose Bowl. They lost to Washington 17-7, but held on to the national championship since at that time voting for the national championship was completed before the bowl games were played.

1960 SEASON RECORD 8-2-0
BIG TEN CONFERENCE RECORD 6-1-0

September 24	Minnesota 26	Nebraska 14	(at Nebraska)
October 1	Minnesota 42	Indiana 0	
October 8	Minnesota 7	Northwestern 0	
October 15	Minnesota 21	Illinois 10	

October 22	Minnesota 10	Michigan 0	(at Michigan)
October 29	Minnesota 48	Kansas State 7	
November 5	Minnesota 27	Iowa 10	
November 12	Minnesota 14	Purdue 23	
November 19	Minnesota 26	Wisconsin 7	(at Wisconsin)
January 2	Minnesota 7	Washington 17	(at Rose Bowl in Pasedena)

The 1960 national champions had guard Tom Brown achieve All-American status, and Brown also won the Outland Trophy that year. He was later elected to the College Football Hall of Fame. Brown and end Tom Hall were also voted All-Big Ten players in 1960.

From 1934 through the 1960 season, the Gophers won 6 national championships. Gopher football, however, has not been able to get back to the glory of those championship seasons, and it has been very hard on loyal Gopher followers.

The Gophers began the 2003 season with six consecutive wins, including a monumental 20-14 win at Penn State before 106,735. The next week, looking for win number seven, the Gophers played Michigan at home before 62, 374 at the Metrodome in one of the biggest games in decades.

It started on a wonderful note with the Gophers taking a massive 35-14 lead only to fall to a Wolverine rally, losing by a final score of 38-35. It was devastating to the Golden Gophers but perhaps more so to the fans, who had waited so long for this promising season. To have Michigan on the ropes only to lose seemed to do them in.

The next week against Michigan State attendance fell to 38, 778. The six-win Gophers lost, and once again many believers were disillusioned.

But each fall hope springs eternal. And with the arrival of head coach Tim Brewster and his positive outlook, the hope that the Gophers will once again return to national prominence is alive.

3

BELL AND ELLER

They were All-Big Ten players, All-Americans, and College and Pro Football Hall of Famers.

They each won numerous awards and are in the conversation about the greatest defensive players to ever play the game of football.

And they played together on the same line for the University of Minnesota Golden Gophers and proudly wore the maroon and gold.

Their names: Bobby Bell and Carl Eller.

The beginning of the 1960 season ushered in a feeling that the Gophers were ready for a successful campaign. Maybe it was the thought that the team couldn't do much worse than the previous two years, during which the Gophers notched only three wins.

Perhaps it was the belief that there were some players on this 1960 Golden Gopher squad who were about to do something special.

One of them was Bobby Bell. I don't think anyone knew just exactly how special he was. At least those sitting in the stands, watching on television or listening on the radio weren't in on what he was going to bring to the Gophers as he approached his sophomore year.

Minnesota recruited Bobby Bell out of Shelby, North Carolina, as a quarterback, and he became a two-time All-American tackle for the Gophers, and also won the prestigious Outland Trophy as the best collegiate lineman in 1962.

The transition Bell made from quarterback to offensive lineman was given great accolades by all who followed Minnesota football, especially the media. In addition to the Outland Award, Bell received a Big Ten conference Most Valuable Player award, and was a third place finisher in the Heisman Trophy voting.

Bell led the Gophers to a 22-6-1 overall record, and was also the first African-American player on the Gopher basketball squad. Bell was not only a tremendous football player but a great all-around athlete.

Bell was an exceptional high school athlete, playing halfback on a six-man football team for a then-segregated school.

During his junior season, he went to the quarterback position and received All-State honors on his now-converted eleven-man squad. His play at Minnesota is legendary, and he is remembered as one of the greatest all around athletes to ever step on the gridiron. Bell used his athletic prowess to play halfback and quarterback in high school, tackle at Minnesota and linebacker for the Kansas City Chiefs.

Bell may have been one of the most gifted linebackers to ever play the professional game. It was reported that he once ran a 40-yard dash in 4.5 seconds. He was noted as one of the most physically able linebackers in professional football history, with tremendous speed and size.

His 6'4" and 230 pound frame and his open field tackling ability rank him as one of the best to ever play the game. If on the rare occasion he would miss a tackle, he had the incredible speed to make up for the miss and still make the tackle on the play.

Bell was also known in the professional ranks as a great blitzing player from the outside linebacker position. He recorded 40 career quarterback sacks and likely would have had more, except for the fact that his position was designed more for pass coverage than rushing the quarterback.

Hank Stram, his coach in Kansas City, once said about Bobby Bell, "Bobby could have played all 22 positions on the field and played them well."

During his pro football career, Bell intercepted 26 passes and scored six touchdowns on the takeovers, and also scored on an on-side kick and on two fumble recoveries. His desire to play the game, even when injured, became legendary, and his passion for the game was second to none.

Upon finishing his collegiate career with the Gophers, Bell was drafted by the Minnesota Vikings and the Kansas City Chiefs, and chose to start his professional career in the old American Football League with Kansas City.

He was an eight-time All Pro for the Chiefs. In 1983 Bell was elected into the Pro Football Hall of Fame and followed that up with selection to the College Football Hall of Fame and the All-AFL team as well.

Some would argue that Bobby Bell was the greatest Gopher ever.

Some would even make the argument that he may have been the greatest defensive player to ever play the game. He certainly was the most decorated lineman of the 1962 college football season. He did things on the football field during his years at Minnesota that had rarely been seen before. He was strong, agile and incredibly quick.

"From the very first time that I saw him, I knew he was special," said Gopher coach Murray Warmath. "He was bigger, faster, and made plays that others could not make. We knew right from the beginning when we started recruiting him that he was an outstanding football player. We never once had a doubt."

"Bobby was about 220-225 pounds and was extremely quick. He was and still is a real gentleman and a fine person. We knew that then and he has lived up to it every day while at the University of Minnesota, and since his collegiate career ended. Bobby Bell was the kind of person who always wanted to do the right thing. We knew he would play right away because of his ability," said Warmath.

"We recruited him to Minnesota as a quarterback but knew right from the beginning that Bobby Bell could play any position. The first day he came in and looked at the roster and couldn't find his name under the quarterbacks. We told him to look under the tackle position. It didn't matter to Bobby, he just wanted to play and loved to hit people," said Warmath.

"I am forever appreciative for what Coach Warmath did for me," recalls Bell. "Everyone thought he was crazy to bring black athletes north, but I am sure glad he did. I had the opportunity to go to a great school like Minnesota and Coach Warmath gave me the chance."

"Every time I come into town, I try to make the time to go and see him, and I am always thrilled by it," says Bell.

"It was such a new experience for me to come north to play football. I had never played with white kids before. I had never been on an airplane. I was from a small school and we played 6-man football. It was a real culture shock for me. I was at Minnesota not just for me but for my family, my friends and for others to have the opportunity," reflects Bell.

"I just wanted to play and I didn't care what position I played. I was recruited to come to Minnesota as a quarterback. When I went to look

Bobby Bell

at the roster before practice, I didn't see my name with the other quarterbacks. I looked at the fullbacks and the halfbacks and still didn't see my name. It scared me because I thought for a minute that I was off the team and would have to leave. Assistant Coach Denver Crawford came by and told me to look at the tackle position, and that's where I found my name," said Bell. "I didn't care, I just wanted to play."

"Coach Crawford was very helpful to me. I asked him one day if he would help me because I knew absolutely nothing about the tackle position. He worked with me after practices and really taught me the position," recalls Bell. "I would have done anything to play. I just wanted to be on the field. I didn't want to let people down."

"Although there were many unforgettable Bell moments, there is one I will always remember," Warmath recalls. "It was the Purdue game in 1960. It was a vicious, hard-hitting game and Bobby had been injured in the first half of the game. His father had traveled up from North Carolina to see him play."

"At half time, Bobby had taken his uniform off and was in the training room and really hurting. There was a knock on the door and his father came in and said to Bobby, 'I didn't come all the way up here from North Carolina to see you get hurt, so put your clothes back on.' And he did and led us out for the second half," recalls Warmath.

"I have never seen in all my years in football a more perfect player. He did everything we ever asked of him on a football field and much, much more. I truly love Bobby Bell. He was such a great player and is such a great person also," said Warmath.

"He was the best athlete that I have ever seen," said Bob Stein, former Gopher and All-American in 1967 and 1968, who played with Bell when they were both with the Kansas City Chiefs.

"He was an incredible athlete. He could excel at anything he tried. I have seen him catch flies right out of the air, throw a football farther than quarterbacks, and beat some of the NFL's fastest players in foot races," said Stein.

"Bobby was tough and he was smart and he would never allow himself to be timed in the 40 yard dash," Stein recalled. "He did not want anyone to know how fast he was in training camp or at any other time because if he were timed, then people would know his speed, and they would never race him for some friendly coin. So he was never timed and he always won the races," laughs Stein.

When Bobby Bell won the Outland Trophy in 1962, Coach Warmath called him "the greatest lineman I have ever seen."

It's no wonder that Gopher head football coach Tim Brewster talks about the contributions of Bobby Bell to the Gopher football program. "I am in regular contact with Bobby," says Coach Brewster. "He means so much to the Gopher program. He was such a tremendous football player and is such a wonderful person. He may be the greatest defensive player of all time."

***

During much of the time Bell wore the maroon and gold, the Gopher roster also included Carl Eller, who came along one year later and played two seasons on the same Gopher team with Bell.

Carl Eller was a tremendous football player. When Eller left the Gophers and began his career with the Minnesota Vikings, he amazed many with his abilities at the pro level as he added to what he had accomplished in the collegiate ranks.

"He did things on the football field that I have never seen before," said the great Fran Tarkenton, former Vikings quarterback.

"I saw him literally pick people up and throw them aside like they were mannequins. He had tremendous speed and quickness and was just absolutely unbelievable. I really liked Carl and thought he was regal on the football field. He was really special," recalls Tarkenton.

Eller was extraordinary as a Golden Gopher. Carl played for Murray Warmath from 1961-1963, two years on the line with Bobby Bell. Think of that. Two of the greatest players to ever play at the collegiate and professional ranks playing on the same Gopher line. Unbelievable!

Carl Eller was a phenomenal player. He was big, strong and tremendously quick. Warmath thought Eller had exceptional abilities and found that, like Bell, Eller dominated on both sides of the line.

Eller was recruited by the Gophers out of Winston-Salem, North Carolina. Eller was so strong and so durable that during his first year with the Gophers he played with a broken hand, after tossing aside the cast that he had been wearing in practices leading up to the game.

He was a dominant leader on the field and played a huge role in the great 21-3 win over UCLA in the 1962 Rose Bowl game. Eller was also an All-American tackle for the Gophers in 1963 and was the runner-up in the voting for the heralded Outland Trophy that same year.

Eller had a massive frame, standing at 6'6" tall and weighing 260 pounds. After finishing his college career at Minnesota, he was drafted in the first round of the NFL draft by the Minnesota Vikings, the sixth overall pick of the draft.

His career with the Vikings spanned 15 years and he also played for one season in Seattle. He played in 225 regular season professional games, was twice named the NFL's Most Valuable Defensive Lineman and played in four Super Bowls while earning All-Pro recognition six times.

While with the Vikings, Eller amassed 130 quarterback sacks and recovered an astounding 23 fumbles. Eller was ultimately elected to both the College Football Hall of Fame and the Pro Football Hall of Fame and will go down in Gopher lore as one of the greatest players to ever put on the maroon and gold uniform.

"I knew he was going to be a great player the first time I ever saw him," said former Gopher coach Murray Warmath. "He had great capabilities and was so incredibly fast for such a big man."

Warmath lights up when talking about Eller, and the gleam in his eye grows brighter when speaking of Eller and Bell on the same squad.

"Carl was a real pleasure to coach," says Warmath. "The University of Minnesota was very blessed to have had him play for us. He was a real gentleman. Carl always gave 100%, and he had a tremendous desire to be successful in practice and in games. He was so beautifully qualified to play the game."

"I still see him from time to time and it is always a pleasure for me when I get the opportunity to talk with him. Like Bobby Bell, I truly love the both of them very much. They are the perfect examples of the fact that players win games, the coaches do not," says Warmath.

As a Viking, Carl was a part of the famed Purple People Eaters, one of the greatest defensive lines in pro football history.

Bobby Bell and Carl Eller were both magnificent high school players, excelled to the highest of standards and levels while athletes at the University of Minnesota, and continued to excel in the professional

Carl Eller

ranks.

It's no wonder that current Gopher head coach Tim Brewster calls Bell and Eller "arguably the greatest defensive players who ever played the game."

4

GREATEST GOPHERS OF ALL TIME

It is difficult to fathom a listing of Gopher greats of the past because there have been so many. In the early 1950s the legendary names of Paul Giel and Bob McNamara were celebrated as they each reached All-American status. But there were many memorable players that came before them and many afterward.

In 1941 Bruce Smith won the Heisman Trophy, becoming the only Gopher football player to achieve the distinguished honor. Smith was an outstanding running back, leading Minnesota to two national championship seasons under Coach Bernie Bierman in 1940 and 1941.

An interesting story is told about Bruce Smith and his father, Lucius Smith, who also played for the Gophers. In 1910, an undefeated Gopher squad was playing at Michigan for the national championship. Lucius played tackle and kicker for Minnesota. In a hard-fought battle, Michigan prevailed by a score of 6-0 and won the national championship.

Lucius Smith was devastated by the loss and blamed himself for allowing Michigan to take the victory from the Gophers. During the game Lucius substituted for injured players and found himself playing at an unfamiliar position. Noting his assignment, the Wolverines ran a play over him for the winning score. Legend has it that after the game Lucius proclaimed that someday he would have a son who would play for the Gophers and avenge the Michigan loss.

Thirty years later on a muddy, rain-soaked field at Memorial Stadium, Lucius' son, Bruce Smith, stepped on to the field to play against Michigan, in a game that later determined the national championship.

The undefeated Gophers trailed by an identical 6-0 score with Michigan moving toward the Gopher goal line late in the game. Gopher

Bob Paffrath intercepted an errant Wolverine pass in the end zone, and the Gophers took possession on their own twenty yard line. On the first play from scrimmage, Bruce Smith took a reverse hand off, went around and through seven Michigan defenders, and traveled 80 yards for a touchdown. The Gophers' Joe Mernik converted the extra point and Minnesota defeated Michigan 7-6. The Gophers went on that year to capture their fourth national championship.

First hand confirmation of one of the great stories in Gopher football history comes from June Smith, sister of the legendary Heisman Trophy winner. Past accounts of the game mention that Lucius has denied that he ever said that he would someday have a son to avenge the Michigan loss, and June Smith does not recall her father ever saying it. But both June and her father were in the stands in 1940 and did see Bruce run the 80 yards for the winning score.

"I remember the play very well," says June. "Bruce got the ball and plodded right through the mud, around several players, and then all of a sudden he was out in front of every one and went the 80 yards for the touchdown. It was a tremendous game and a win over Michigan, who had the great Tommy Harmon on their team."

June Smith absolutely beams when talking about her brother, Bruce.

"He was a very selfless person," she says. "He never talked about himself. He had great athletic ability and mom and dad were very proud of him. He was just a very nice person and did so many nice things for other people," says June.

Smith was a courageous man and was recognized as such. During a game against Iowa in 1941, he had been held out due to a knee injury. After convincing Coach Bernie Bierman to put him in the game, he set up three of the Gopher touchdowns by his ball carrying skills, leading them to a 34-13 win.

Later, his determined fight against cancer prolonged his life, though he eventually succumbed to the disease in 1967 at the age of 47.

Smith was more than just a football player. He was a kind and gentle man who, even in the last stages of his life, his body riddled by cancer, took on the challenge of visiting many hospitalized cancer patients. His inspirational support of others resulted in Father William Cantwell pro-

Bruce Smith

posing that Bruce Smith be recognized for sainthood.

Father Cantwell, who knew nothing of Smith's greatness on the grid-iron, made the proposal based on what he had seen from Smith over the few short months near the end of Smith's life. Father Cantwell proclaimed the following in a statement to the National Catholic News Service: "Because he lived a life of heroic value and because of the way he died, Smith deserves to be canonized."

Smith's memorable run against Michigan will, for many Gopher fans, always be associated with the infamous "Armistice Day Blizzard" which hit just 48 hours after the game ended. The 64,000 fans in Memorial Stadium watched a historic Gopher-Wolverine battle as the storm rolled in from the west.

The Minnesota team that day faced the likes of Herbert "Fritz" Crisler, heralded Michigan coach returning to the Twin Cities after once coaching the Gopher eleven, setting the stage for a showdown between the two undefeated teams. The Gophers' 7-6 victory proved to be the only loss that year for Michigan. It was only fitting to have Smith put his brilliant touch on the game's ending.

Smith was a great high school player from Faribault, Minnesota, where he was a four-year letterman in football, basketball, and golf. He came to Minnesota in the fall of 1938, had an outstanding freshman year, and then became a regular on the football team in the 1939 season, sharing honors with another great Gopher player, George Franck.

The Smith touchdown against bitter rival Michigan is well-known to the maroon and gold faithful as the greatest touchdown run in Gopher history. Smith wore number 54 at Minnesota and it became the first number ever to be retired by the Gophers.

Bruce Smith's legacy goes far deeper than football. A 1941 film based on Smith's life was released by Columbia Pictures under the title *Smith of Minnesota*. The film starred Bruce Smith playing himself. Promotional material for the film read, "Bruce Smith attended the University of Minnesota from 1937 to 1941, the only Gopher football player to ever win the Heisman Trophy, college football's highest honor. He was an A student and a devout Catholic, who lived by 'an hour a day for God' throughout his life. He was in church before and after every football game, no matter the score. A natural leader and example, he was team captain his senior year. Faith helped him through all life's transitions:

Smith is the only Heisman Trophy winner in Minnesota history.

marriage, a father of four, stricken with cancer and dying in 1967, he maintained his humility, service to others, and faithfulness to the end. Many who knew him acclaimed him a saint; his cause is being considered."

A book about Bruce Smith, titled *The Game Breaker*, was written by Tom Akers and published in 1977. Within the pages is a tribute to Bruce Smith by the Reverend William J. Cantwell, which appeared in the *Catholic Bulletin* of September 1967:

The game of football means different things to different people. It is one sport which very quickly separates the weak from the strong, the boys from the men. Like other sports, football has its own language: the blitz, the bomb, red-dogging, clipping, screening, scrambling …. these are but a few of the basic words of the gridiron vocabulary.

Football fans, coaches and sports writers are most anxious to praise and reward the real heroes of this game. And this is the only way it should be. In college football each year the highest honor given to the outstanding player in the nation is the Heisman Trophy. No other award is as valuable as this one. The Heisman Trophy does for a football player what the Congressional Medal of Honor does for a soldier. It sets him apart from the rest of the men.

Only one player from the University of Minnesota has won the Heisman Trophy. He did so 26 years ago. His name is Bruce Smith. Bruce Smith died on Monday, August 28, 1967, after a long fight with cancer. He was only 47 years old, happily married, and the father of four children.

I never saw Bruce Smith play football, but he and I were friends. I met him for the first time several months ago on a Friday afternoon while making the rounds of the Catholic patients at St. Barnabas Hospital. I had no idea who he was. I knew nothing about his fame as a football player.

Friday after Friday I would visit him. We talked of many things, from the strangeness of the weather to the bitterness of the war. I met his father and his brother, and his brave wife, Gloria. This man loved his family. How much he desired to be with his wife and their four children, to get back on his feet again.

Bruce Smith did not tell me that he had won the Heisman Trophy. He was not that kind of man. In fact, it was by accident that another patient at the hospital told me who this good man on the fifth floor was. When I did find out, I was not the least bit surprised.

For Bruce Smith was a real champion all the way down the line. He stood head and shoulders over most men that I have met. You could see it immediately. This man had that certain something that God bestows on only a few men in each generation. Although he was sick and as uncomfortable as any patient at the hospital, he did not complain or find fault or lose patience. He was a Christian optimist with the guts and courage of an All-American. He was everyone's favorite patient at the hospital, in the same way he had been everyone's favorite player at the University Saturday after Saturday for three seasons in a row. Everyone was pulling for him.

The best minds in medical science did all they could to keep this man alive.

His desire for life was as strong as any man's and far stronger than most. But cancer is no respecter of persons. It strikes the young and the old, the weak and the strong, men, women and children.

Since first reading the headline "Bruce Smith of Football Fame Dies of Cancer" in Monday evening's newspaper, I have thought of this man many times. Frequently I have petitioned our Heavenly Father in his behalf .... that he may quickly enjoy that place of refreshment, light, and peace that was prepared for him for all eternity.

In the Gospel of today's Mass our Lord gives us a word picture of a wedding banquet and the reactions of the invited guests as to who shall sit in the first place. The same Jesus came to serve and not to be served, and who said, 'Learn of Me because I am meek and humble of heart,' actually giving us a picture of the perfect joy and happiness of Heaven.

I believe our own Lord's words, 'He who humbles himself shall be exalted,' describes very well Bruce Smith of Minnesota as he entered his Father's House to begin eternal life.

Bruce never really left the home he loved. He rests in Fort Snelling Memorial Cemetery on the bluff above the Mississippi. It is not a great distance from that huge brick stadium to the north where the great roar of crowds still spills over the rim into the crisp brilliance of autumn. Those who come here in their youth will have their latter day idols, and this is as it should be. Others, those with gray in their locks, will come to see if there ever will be another like the one they once saw, a man who was called "The Game Breaker," a man named Smith.

--Reverend William J. Cantwell, CSP

***

On November 3, 1908, in Rainy River, Ontario, Canada, just over one hundred years ago, Bronislau "Bronko" Nagurski was born. Nagurski went on to great fame as a football player for the University of Minnesota. He certainly had the name and the passion to play the game, and all who were fortunate to have seen him play in the collegiate and professional ranks may have seen the best football player who ever lived.

Nagurski was a special player and a huge man. Bronko at one time held the record-and likely still does-for having the largest ring size in National Football League, an astounding 19.5 inches (86 mm inside circumference.)

Nagurski was one of the largest running backs of the time. He had a great collegiate career with the Gophers and professionally with the Chicago Bears. Bronko also had an incredible professional wrestling career and spent the last years of his life running a gas station in International Falls, Minnesota.

The recipient of many honors for his outstanding football career, Bronko especially treasured a tribute from the town of International Falls, the creation of the Bronko Nagurski Museum in Smokey Bear Park.

***

When it comes to great Gophers of the past, you have to include one of the legendary coaches, Henry L. Williams, who was the head coach at Minnesota from 1900-1921. Williams' record of 136 wins, 33 losses and 11 ties places him in a category by himself. He was one of the greatest college football coaches of all time.

Williams is credited with being the first to bring winning football to the state of Minnesota. He was an originator of many aspects of the game that we still see today, and he will go down as one of the real pioneers of the game. The 1941 national title trophy was named after him.

***

The College Football Hall of Fame has recognized Smith, Nagurski and Coach Williams, but there are many other legendary figures who took the field wearing the maroon and gold.

One of the greatest to wear the uniform was Bert Baston, a First Team All-American for the Gophers in 1915 and again in 1916. Baston was from St. Louis Park, Minnesota, and was a leader on the 1915 co-Big Ten championship team under Coach Henry Williams.

***

In 1926 and 1927, the Gophers were blessed with an incredible fullback by the name of Herb Joesting. Joesting played the position from 1925-1927, earning All-American honors the latter two seasons. He was

The legendary Bronco Nagurski.

nicknamed "The Owatonna Thunderbolt" and later played on the Chicago Bears' championship team of 1932.

***

Bernie Bierman led the great national championship teams of 1934-1936. Playing tackle for Bierman on those magnificent teams and earning All-American recognition for the years 1935-1936 was the great Gopher player Ed Widseth. Widseth grew up on a dairy farm in Crookston, Minnesota. While playing for the Gophers he was said to have "lived" in the opposing team's backfield. Widseth was captain and a Most Valuable Player for the Gophers, and played on the championship teams that amassed a 24-1 record during the three seasons that Widseth played. In addition to playing football for the Gophers, Widseth was an outstanding baseball player. After his career at Minnesota, Widseth went on to play professionally for the New York Giants from 1937-1940, earning All-Pro recognition three times. Later, Widseth served as head football coach at the University of St. Thomas for two seasons, leading the Tommies to two conference titles.

***

In 1941 and 1942, the Gophers boasted another All-American in tackle Dick Wildung. Following his collegiate career, Wildung played professionally for the Green Bay Packers and is in the Packers Hall of Fame. Wildung was born in Anoka, Minnesota, and died in 2006 at the age of 84.

***

One of the more famous players recalled with the greats of Gopher football is mentioned not only because of his star-studded status as a football player, but because of the appropriateness of his name. Francis "Pug" Lund, from Rice Lake, Wisconsin, ignited the 1934 championship season for the Gophers with an incredible scoring pass against Pittsburgh on a late fourth-down play. During that season, Lund averaged almost six yards per carry and was also known for his ferocious blocking style.

Francis "Pug" Lund

Pug Lund was as tough a player as they come, and, according the College Football Hall of Fame records, Coach Bierman once claimed that "Lund was our spark plug. He was battered and broken up, teeth knocked out, finger amputated, and thumb broken, and through all that he carried on."

Lund earned All-American honors in 1933 and 1934. He also participated in track and field for Minnesota. Lund had many opportunities to play professional football but chose a career in the automotive insurance industry.

***

During the 1909 season, the Gophers were quarterbacked by Johnny McGovern from Arlington, Minnesota. Johnny was an All-American in 1909, though he stood only five feet nine inches tall and weighed 155 pounds. He was not only a great quarterback but also an outstanding kicker for the Gophers. Playing three varsity seasons, McGovern missed only one game, notably playing the entire game in a loss to Wisconsin with a broken collarbone. He was a tough and gritty player who never gave up against larger and more formidable opponents.

Johnny McGovern was not only a great quarterback but also an outstanding kicker.

Ed Rogers

***

In 1876 in Libby, Minnesota, another Gopher College Football Hall of Famer—Eddie Rogers—was born. Rogers would go on to star for the Gophers during the 1901-1903 seasons. Rogers was an end and a kicker for the Gophers and earned the Hall of Fame recognition in 1968. He also played college football at the Carlisle Indian Industrial School. Rogers was one of the great University of Minnesota team captains, and was a key player in the Minnesota tie against Michigan in 1903, which became known as the Little Brown Jug game. Rogers kicked the tying extra point on the last play of the game. When he left the Gophers and went to Carlisle, he also became the school's football coach. After his career in football, Rogers practiced law for over six decades and in 1963 he was named the national Outstanding County Attorney.

***

The early days of Gopher football also include Gopher great Bobby Marshall. Marshall was born in Milwaukee, Wisconsin, and played at Minnesota from 1904-1906. He graduated from Minneapolis Central High School and became one of the first outstanding players at Minnesota. He once recorded a 60-yard field goal in the rain on a muddy field to beat the University of Chicago 4-2, when field goals counted four points.

Bobby Marshall was the first African-American to play in the Big Nine Conference, later to be called the Big Ten Conference, and shared the honor as a National Football League player. He played with several

local professional teams after graduation and also spent from 1920-1924 in
the NFL.

While recognized at Minnesota for
his accomplishments on the football
field, Marshall was also an outstanding baseball player and a sprinter on
the track team.

Bobby Marshall

***

Minnesota has always been proud
of the collegiate career of the great
San Francisco 49er and professional
wrestler Leo Nomellini. Born in
Lucca, Italy, Nomellini, the two-time
All-American, never missed a game in
14 seasons of professional football
with the 49ers. He was a tackle/guard with the Gophers and was a legendary figure in both the college and professional ranks. His wrestling
career earned him championship recognition under the name "Leo the
Lion."

***

During the 1951-1953 seasons, the Gophers managed a disappointing
record of 10-13-4. Yet during these dismal campaigns, the Gophers had
in their backfield one of the greatest runners of all time. A young man
from Winona, Minnesota, by the name of Paul Giel wore the famous
Number 10.

Paul Giel was one of the most dynamic ball carriers to ever put on a
Gopher uniform. Giel was the Big Ten Conference Most Valuable Player
twice, and was the runner up for the Heisman Trophy in 1953, behind
Notre Dame's John Lattner. As a Gopher halfback he achieved All-
American status in 1952 and again in 1953. After being moved from the
quarterback position, which at the time under the single-wing offense
was primarily a blocking position, Giel passed for 123 yards and ran for
113 in his first game.

Perhaps the best game from Giel came in the 50th anniversary of the

#10 Paul Giel

Little Brown Jug game against Michigan. The Gophers had dominated the contests in the early part of the century, but the Gophers had not been in Michigan's class for several years. The October 24, 1953 game proved to be historic. Giel scored two touchdowns and passed for another as the Gophers upset Michigan 22-0 during his senior year.

Facing an undefeated Michigan team as heavy underdogs, the team came together to produce one of the great victories for the maroon and gold. Giel was dominant on the ground and through the air that day, and also provided great defensive play, intercepting two key Michigan passes. Giel finished the afternoon with 35 carries for 112 yards, and threw 13-18 completions for 169 yards. He also ran for 90 yards on kick off returns. He set a new Big Ten record by handling the ball 53 times for the day, culminating in one of the greatest gridiron performances of all time.

Rushing records at Minnesota were held by Giel for over 25 years, solidifying his greatness as a Gopher running back. Giel was also a tremendous baseball player at Minnesota and went on to play professional baseball with the Giants, Pittsburgh Pirates and Minnesota Twins. Later on, he became a local radio celebrity and the athletic director for the University of Minnesota.

***

Following Giel in the backfield was Bob McNamara, number 44. His 89-yard touchdown run to defeat Iowa in 1954 is still legendary in Gopher lore. Bob's love for Minnesota football covers five decades.

"When I was playing for Hastings High School, Bud Grant was always my hero," says Bob. "He made so many great plays for the Gophers. Over the last thirty-five years I have done a lot of fundraising for Minnesota, I have always wanted to do something for the University of Minnesota, because it has done so much for me and my brother Pinky. We were very lucky to have been able to play football here at Minnesota and because we were the only team in town at the time, we were able to get a lot of local publicity. Giving back is important to both of us," says Bob.

"The Minnesota football tradition is matched by few schools. We have six national championships and have had so many great players. What is happening at the University right now is special. It gives me goose bumps to see the new football stadium. It is really something special.

"Another real special feeling for Pinky and me is to have the new Gopher locker room named after Coach Murray Warmath. He deserves the great honor and we are so proud of that as well. He was always like a father figure for us."

"I have so many great memories playing for the Gophers. Before we beat Iowa in 1954, we had lost at Iowa City the previous year," recalls Bob, "and we didn't have facemasks on the helmets then. I remember I took a terrible beating, as if Sonny Liston had worked me over."

The "back to campus" atmosphere the new stadium will provide is special to Bob McNamara.

"We seemed to lose that college warmth that was present before," says Bob. "I will be there on September 12, 2009, for the first game in the new stadium. I will be going with my wife, my brother and Coach Warmath."

Another interesting piece to the Bob McNamara football era relates to the great signal caller for Minnesota back then, named Geno Cappeletti. Geno was a great player and later a star in the old American Football

Bob McNamara picks up some tough yardage.

League. When the first game in the AFL was played in 1960, it featured the Denver Broncos against the Boston Patriots.

Geno Cappelletti of the Patriots made the first kick off in the first game. Bob McNamara made the first kick return in the game. One must wonder if Cappelletti made the first tackle.

***

When the 1960 national championship team is remembered, the name Tom Brown is always mentioned. Brown was one of the greatest defensive and offensive linemen to ever play for the Golden Gophers.

In 1960, Brown won the Outland Trophy, which recognized him as the best collegiate lineman in the country, and was also the Big Ten Conference Most Valuable Player. Brown had a tremendous ability to open holes in the line for ball carriers and was a ferocious tackler on the defensive line.

Brown was named All-American his senior season, and was such a dominant force that he was runner-up in the voting for the Heisman Trophy, receiving the highest ever voting total for an interior lineman, an incredible accomplishment. Brown played professionally in Canada for the British Columbia Lions, where he also received high acclaim and numerous awards. He was voted into the Canadian Football Hall of Fame in 2003.

***

Bobby Cox made the cover of *Sports Illustrated* in 1957, called the best quarterback in the country. He was quite a football player at the University of Minnesota and had quite the unusual background as well. He was born in dire financial straits and ran away from home at the age of 14. While staying with several families in Washington, he was able to complete his education. He was an outstanding athlete in high school at Walla Walla, and won all-state honors in football, basketball and track.

Coach Murray Warmath has been quoted in several places through the years as saying, "I never had anyone who wanted to win more than he did. He was willing to pay the price to be successful."

Cox began his collegiate career at the University of Washington but transferred to Minnesota. In 1956, he led the Golden Gophers to a 6-2-1 record, and the Gophers ended the season ranked number 12 in the final

AP poll.

***

Clayton Tonnemaker, another great lineman for Minnesota, played from 1946-1949 on the same line with the great Leo Nomelinni. Tonnemaker, who was born in Ogilvie, Minnesota, was team captain in 1949 and was also voted All-American. After his collegiate career ended, Tonnemaker played for the Green Bay Packers from 1950-1954.

***

Born in Davenport, Iowa, George Henning "Sonny" Franck was half-back for the Gophers from 1938-1940. He was a terrific player and became a first round draft pick following college. Franck was an incredible running back for the Gophers and also starred on the Minnesota track team, recording a 9.6 in the 100 yard dash. Franck played on the undefeated Gopher team that won the 1940 national championship; he was third in the voting for the Heisman that year.

***

Frank "Butch" Larson comes to mind when you think of one of the most dominating ends to ever play for Minnesota. Larson was named an All-American in 1933 and 1934, playing under head coach Bernie Bierman. Selected for the East-West Shrine game, Larson was the room-mate of future president Gerald Ford, who was a Michigan Wolverine.

Larson was a great player noted for his hard hitting and punt coverage. After his Minnesota career concluded, he coached in college and in the Canadian Football League. He led the Winnipeg Blue Bombers to the Grey Cup in 1950.

***

Another All-American from the undefeated 1934 Gophers national championship team was guard Bill Bevan. Bevan played high school football at St. Paul Central. He was a powerful force on the Gopher line and was also a kicker on the squad, scoring 38 PATs. During his time with the Gophers, Bevan became noted as one of the toughest linemen in the country. He used his toughness to earn a Big Ten conference light heavyweight boxing title. After completing his college career, Bevan went on to become a college football coach and later a volunteer high school coach.

***

Bierman's teams in the mid-thirties not only won national championships but also produced some incredible football players. One of those players was Sheldon Biese. Biese was known as one of the best blockers of his era. He was noted for his ability to open gaping holes for "Pug" Lund, part of the Gopher backfield at the time. During the three years that Biese played for the Gophers, their record was spotless, never losing a football game. After graduation, Biese became a college football coach at Holy Cross, St. Thomas and back at Minnesota.

***

One of the most notable Minnesotans due to his career at Minnesota and as coach of the Minnesota Vikings is Harry "Bud" Grant. Named by Gophers head football coach Tim Brewster as perhaps the greatest all-around athlete to ever attend Minnesota, Grant finished his collegiate career with a total of nine varsity letters, three each in football, basketball and baseball.

Grant, born and raised in Superior, Wisconsin, earned All-Big Ten recognition twice as an end on the football field. Grant actually beat out Bruce Smith and Bronko Nagurski in the voting as the University of Minnesota's Top Athlete for the first 50 years of the century.

Following his collegiate career, Grant played professional basketball for the Minneapolis Lakers, professional football for the Philadelphia Eagles and played and coached professionally in Canada. He led the Winnipeg Blue Bombers to four Grey Cup championships and later had a successful career as the head coach of the Minnesota Vikings, where his teams earned 11 Central Division championships and made four Super Bowl appearances. He was elected to the Pro Football Hall of Fame in 1994, and is also a member of the Canadian Football Hall of Fame.

***

The list goes on and on and there are many not yet mentioned players who have achieved All-American status while playing football for the

Golden Gophers. Many of these great athletes will be in the College Football Hall of Fame in the future, and will be recognized for their phenomenal achievements. Two-time All-Americans like Loren Solem (1913-14), Bob Stein (1967-68), Tyrone Carter (1998-99), Ben Hamilton (1999-2000) and Greg Eslinger (2004-05) were great players and are headed for recognition in the future.

In addition to the great careers of some Gophers, the following group went on to be recognized as members of the Pro Football Hall of Fame: Bronko Nagurski in 1963; Leo Nomellini in 1969; Bobby Bell in 1983; Bud Grant in 1994; Carl Eller in 1994; and Charlie Sanders in 2007.

***

Minnesota has had some great players through the years and many of them have been quarterbacks. Going back to the last national championship season of 1960, the Gophers were led by Sandy Stephens. Johnny McGovern quarterbacked the maroon and gold from 1908-1910, and was elected into the College Football Hall of Fame. And there were others who may not have achieved the honors, but were highly regarded signal callers.

When it comes to passing, the greatest quarterback in Gopher history is Bryan Cupito, who led the Gophers from 2003 to 2006. Cupito amassed more passing yardage than any Minnesota player ever. During his four years leading the Gophers, he attempted 918 passes and

Bryan Cupito is the all-time career passing yardage leader at Minnesota.

completed 513 for 7446 total yards. He also threw for 55 touchdowns.

Second on the list of all time passers is Cory Sauter, who played for Minnesota from 1994 to 1997. During Sauter's years, he passed for 6834 yards and threw for 40 touchdowns. Almost all of Cupito's and Sauter's passing achievements came during their last three years of eligibility, as neither played very much during his first year with the Gophers. In fact, Cupito threw only one pass in 2003 and it was incomplete.

Next in line of all time greatest passers are Asad Abdul-Khaliq (2000-2003), Adam Weber (2007-) and Marquel Fleetwood (1989-1992).

The final five in the Gophers top ten quarterbacks with respect to passing records are Rickie Fogge (1984-1987); Mike Hohensee (1981-1982); Tim Shade (1993-1994); Tony Dungy (1973-1976); and Billy Cockerham (1996-1999).

***

When it comes to carrying the football, the Gophers have also been represented well. Many great running backs have blasted through the line for the Gophers. Bruce Smith, Minnesota's only Heisman Trophy winner, was one of the best ever, as was Paul Giel, Bob McNamara and a host of others. Greats like Bronko Nagurski ran with the football to All-

Darrell Thompson rushed for 4,654 yards and 40 touchdowns during his Gopher career.

American and College Football Hall of Fame status. Herb Joesting was another carrying the honors of All-American and Hall of Famer. George Franck holds both honors for the Gophers as well, along with the great Francis "Pug" Lund.

The all time rusher in Golden Gopher history is Darrell Thompson, currently a Gopher radio game day analyst. Thompson carried the football from 1986 to 1989 for the Gophers. He was given the ball 936 times and ran for 4,654 yards, a little over 46 football fields. Thompson scored 40 touchdowns during his incredible career.

Second on the list of all time rushers is Laurence Maroney (2003-2005) with 660 carries for a total of 3,933 yards and 32 scores. Third comes Thomas Hamner (1996-1999); Marion Barber (2001-2004); Chris Darkins (1992-1995); Marion Barber (1977- 1980); Tellis Redmond (1999-2001); Amir Pinnix (2004-2007); Gary White (1977-1980); and Francis "Pug" Lund (1932-1934).

***

Many other Gophers are worthy of mention. Gino Cappelletti played for the Gophers from 1952-1954, and became the all time American Football League leading scorer. Phil Bengston was a Gopher player from 1932-1934 and later became an assistant and head football coach in the National Football League. Gil Dobie played from 1899-1901 and led the Cornell football team to two national championships. Tony Dungy played quarterback for Minnesota from 1974-1976 and won a Super Bowl as the coach of the Indianapolis Colts. Vern Gagne lettered in 1943 and went on to become a professional wrestling champion. Bud Wilkinson, a Gopher on the national championship teams under Bernie Bierman from 1934-1936, went on to coach at Oklahoma where he won three national championships.

In addition, Minnesota has had three Outland Trophy winners, honoring the nation's best collegiate lineman: Tom Brown in 1960, Bobby Bell in 1962 and Greg Esslinger in 2005. Tyrone Carter won the Jim Thorp award in 1999; Bernie Bierman won the Amos Alonzo Stagg Award in 1958, and in 1960 Murray Warmath won the Eddie Robinson Coach of the Year Award and the Paul "Bear" Bryant Award. In 2005, Greg Esslinger won the Dave Rimington Award for the nation's best center, and in 2006 Matt Spaeth won the John Mackey Award as the best tight end. In 1999, former Gopher Glen Mason won the Dave McClain Coach of the Year Award. The coveted Chicago Tribune Silver Football Award went to Biggie Munn in 1931, Francis "Pug" Lund in 1934, Paul Giel in 1952 and again in 1953, Tom Brown in 1960, and Sandy Stephens in 1961.

Greg Esslinger won the 2005 Dave Rimington Award as the nation's best center.

5

VOICES AND SOUNDS OF GOLDEN GOPHER FOOTBALL

"University regulations prohibit the use of intoxicating beverages within the stadium confines. Ushers have been authorized to REFUSE admission to ticket holders who are intoxicated."

The boos from the crowd, particularly from the student section, would almost drown out the final words from legendary public address announcer Jules Perlt, as he made the requisite pre-game announcement.

Jules Perlt was a voice like none other. He represented Minnesota Golden Gopher football as much as anyone who ever coached or played. His voice resonated throughout Memorial Stadium.

"CLIPPING penalty against MinnesoooTA."

"The pass, Hankinson to ANNNDerrrrr…son makes it a first down at the TWELLLLVVVVE."

"BeLLLLLL in on the tackle."

"BOMBidieRRR in for MINNesota."

"VANNNNN de Walker in to punt for MINNesoooTA"

Jules Perlt's voice was riveting, and it was the voice of Golden Gopher football for more than 50 years. Perlt was also a Gopher athlete, lettering in gymnastics in 1923, and he was the gymnastics team coach at Minnesota in 1940, when the Gophers were first in the Big Ten and ranked third in the NCAA.

Anyone who ever attended a Gopher football game will remember how Perlt enunciated the players' names as he gave the lineups and announced the action on the field. Hearing Perlt announce the starting lineups for the 1960 national champion Gophers was unforgettable:

"And now if you will turn to pages 15 and 16 in your *Gopher Goalpost*, we'll give you today's tentative starting lineups"

"Starting for Minnesota at left end number 86, HALL! Left tackle, number 78, BELLLLLL! Left Guard number 68, MulVENA. CENTER; number 55, CAPTAIN Greg Larson..... Right guard, number 33, Hook. Right TACKLE, number 76, Brixius. RIGHT END, number 89, Deegan! QUARTERBACK!! Number 15, Stephens!....Left halfback, number 40, Mulholland. Right halfback, number 28, Munsey. And Fullllllllback,...... number 38, HAGberg!"

Gopher fans got chills up and down their spines when they heard Perlt, and they knew they were ready for the game.

In addition to doing the public address announcing for Gopher football, Jules was the voice for Golden Gopher basketball, hockey and track. But football was where he received the most notoriety, announcing his first game at the Brick House in 1928. He remained in the position until 1987, announcing more than 400 football games and over 1000 basketball games for the University.

In 1996, Jules Perlt became a U of M Distinguished Service Hall of Fame inductee. He was as much a part of Gopher history as if he played for the maroon and gold. He was an original and synonymous with Gopher pride.

***

Taking over for Jules Perlt for ten years was Dick Jonckowski, who is also currently the public address voice for Gopher basketball and baseball. Dick speaks very fondly of Jules Perlt and has always remembered how much Jules helped him when he took over his duties.

"Remember how he called the play by play of the squirrel that ran on to the field before a Gopher game," Jonckowski likes to recall. "And there is a squirrel on the field and he is at the 40, the 30, the 20, the 10, TOUCHDOWN! Classic Jules Perlt."

Jonckowski also remembers a Gopher basketball timeout when Jules was handed something to read over the public address system. And just before he was to read the announcement, the band started playing.

"Will the band please shut up so I can read this announcement," came the legendary voice over the PA system.

The "Polish Eagle" Dick Jonckowski.

Dick Jonckowski, affectionately named "the Polish Eagle," is one of the great Masters of Ceremony. Traveling across the country, he has entertained audiences with his wit, and he loves to make people laugh. One of his greatest passions in life has been the Minnesota Gophers. Having the opportunity to take in his first Gopher football game in 1957, Jonckowski's enduring love for Gopher football has only strengthened as the years have passed. Number 86, Tom Hall, is his all-time favorite player but there are so many others, like brothers Bob and Pinky McNamara.

Bob was an All-American player for the Gophers and both played under Murray Warmath. In 1954, they played together, both running backs and kick returners. One of Jonckowski's favorite stories of Gopher football involves the two.

The Gophers had a couple of kick return plays that year involving the McNamara brothers. If the ball was kicked to Bob, he would approach Pinky, fake a handoff to him, and keep the ball on a fake reverse play. If the ball was kicked to Pinky, he would hand the ball off to Bob on a reverse play.

Bob (#44) and Pinky (#24) McNamara.

One day Pinky tired of either handing the ball to Bob or watching Bob fake the ball to him and keep it, so he approached Coach Warmath and said, "Coach, on our kick return play, it seems as if every time Bob gets the ball, the play is for him to fake the hand off to me and keep the ball, and whenever I receive the kick, I hand it off to Bob. When am I going to be able to fake the hand off to Bob and keep the ball, or when will Bob be able to hand the ball off to me?"

Coach Warmath looked at Pinky and said, "When Bob graduates."

Another of Jonckowski's favorite McNamara stories is when he was a passenger in a car with Bob at the wheel. Bob went through a red light without even a hesitation. When questioned about his lack of concern for the light, Bob said, "Pinky does it all the time and never has any problem."

A few minutes later, Bob went right through another red light without blinking an eye.

Dick again questioned his act.

Bob said, "Pinky does it all the time without any problem."

At the next light, Bob stopped completely even though the light was green.

Dick questioned why he stopped for the green light.

Bob replied, "I think I see Pinky coming."

Jonckowski's early love connection to Gopher football began as a Boy Scout Explorer serving as an usher at Gopher football games. He was always assigned to the bench area and became familiar with many of the greats of the past. He remembers players like Tom Brown, and how he destroyed the Iowa center in the great Gopher-Hawkeye battle of 1960.

"He threw the center right into his own backfield," says Jonckowski, "and it later led to the center snapping the ball over the punter's head on the first series in the game."

"I love the Gophers," says Jonckowski, "and I recall so many of the great players like John Hankinson and what a beautiful pass he threw, and Bobby Bell, what a great player he was. And I remember Tom Teigen's great play on Michigan running back Bennie McRae, which caused a fumble and led to a Gopher win in 1961. And I have seen the play many times and know it well when Bob McNamara returned a punt 89 yards against Iowa, and Pinky actually made three blocks on the play. It was unbelievable!"

Bob McNamara recalls Pinky telling the story and noting his seven blocks that sprung Bob for the 89-yard run. Unbelievable!

Jonckowski's love for Gopher football reminds him of another of his favorite Gopher football stories. It seems one day one of the coaches was looking around the locker room and noticed the name Busted (pronounced Bewstad) was posted on a locker between the lockers of two of his greatest players. The coach had never heard of a player named Busted on his football team.

He angrily hustled to the equipment room where he confronted an unsuspecting equipment manager and said, "I was just looking around the locker room and noticed a locker with the name Busted on it. And it is right between our two All-American players! I want to know who this Busted is, and what is he doing housed between our two greatest players? I don't even know who he is. Can someone explain this to me?"

The equipment manager quickly went with the coach to the locker in question and heard once again from the coach.

"There, right there, there is Busted's locker. WHO IS THIS GUY? I don't know him, can't recall ever seeing him on our squad."

The equipment manager hung his head and replied, "Coach, that is not the locker of a player. There is no Busted. The locker is broken and we put the word busted on it so no one would use it."

The embarrassed head coach said, "Thank you" and turned away mumbling, "Well, good thing I found out because I was going to start Busted on Saturday!"

***

Another legendary Gopher radio voice was the great Ray Christensen, announcing Gopher football and basketball for over 40 years. Ray majored in radio speech at the University of Minnesota and began his broadcasting career in 1946 for the University radio station.

In 1951, he began doing the Gopher football games for WCCO radio and took on basketball as well in 1956. In addition to doing the Gopher football and basketball games, Christensen also did the games for the Minneapolis Lakers, St. Paul Saints baseball team, Minneapolis Millers, Minnesota Twins, and the Minnesota Vikings at various times. Most of his broadcasting career was with WCCO.

In 1995, Ray Christensen was inducted into the U of M Hall of Fame.

Ray Christensen was a great announcer for football and basketball. He made you feel like you were right there with him watching the action. One of his proudest moments was assisting a blind man across 7th Street in downtown Minneapolis. Upon hearing Christensen's voice the blind man said, "You're Ray Christensen, aren't you," and then went on, "Thanks to you, we can really see the games." It was special. Christensen believes that the very best listeners of games are the blind because they are truly seeing what you are telling them.

Perfectionist in preparation would probably be a good way to describe Ray Christensen. He prepared and he was ready to give his very best to tell the listeners what was occurring during the game.

"Do as much work on the microphone as you can and learn to listen," Christensen says, "because when you talk it is going to mean something. Pretend you are talking to one person, not a large group of people.

Henry Morgan, the legendary radio personality, used to say to his listeners, 'Hello anybody,' not everybody," he says. "It is important that you get what you are saying across to one person and then it will work."

Christensen's first year doing the football games for the Gophers was 1951, but he worked for no pay. And he found out that he had the radio broadcast job in an unusual manner. He had applied for the job and was waiting to hear whether he had been selected. With just a week before the first game, he called and was told by athletic director Ike Armstrong's secretary the following: "You can't charge more than $2.50 per meal when on the road doing the games."

The great Ray Christensen.

That was it. Chrstensen had the job and that was probably the quickest selection announcement in history. But the next season, he earned $25 per game.

"I had many great radio partners," said Chrstensen. "I enjoyed working with all of them. I did games with former coach Murray Warmath for a while, and he never acted like a coach. He was a great partner."

"I also worked with former Viking player Paul Flatley for 15 years, and Paul was a great partner. We worked so well together and he was a hard worker. I also enjoyed my work with Paul Giel and the great Gopher Billy Bye."

One of Christensen's fondest memories was the tremendous turnaround from the 1959 losing season to the 1960 championship. Being part of the team's transition from a 2-7 season, last in the Big Ten

Conference, to the national championship was memorable.

"I remember Sandy Stephens, who was the great catalyst for that team. And the incredible Bobby Bell. He was like Adonis, so special. That was such a great time for Gopher football," says Christensen.

"I remember the greatness of Paul Giel and Bob McNamara. And one of my favorite quarterbacks was Mike Hohensee. He was such a great passer."

"Minnesota Gopher football has such great tradition," says Christensen. "Look back at the 1930s, and those great teams of Bernie Bierman. He won those three straight national championships in 1934-1936. And not only were there great players that played for Bierman, but many of them stayed and continue to live here, like Billy Bye and Bud Grant."

"My all-time favorite place to broadcast a game was the Metrodome. It was the most comfortable and we had the most space. It was just an ideal location to do a game. But I had the opportunity to see so many great stadiums, like our old Memorial Stadium, Michigan Stadium and the Ohio State Stadium. They were all special, too."

There was great passion coming from behind the microphone with Ray Christensen, and great thrills when the victories came.

His two favorite games?

"It would have to be the two great Michigan victories," says Christensen.

He speaks of the upsets over the Wolverines in 1986, a 20-17 win on the last second field goal by Chip Lomiller, and the huge win over Michigan in 1977 at Memorial Stadium, 16-0.

He says the 20-17 win in 1986 resulted in "the loudest silence that I ever heard," describing the reaction from the Michigan crowd when the Gophers hit the winning field goal.

Ray Christensen meant so much to Gopher fans for so many years. He is a soft-spoken gentleman; you would never know upon first meeting him that he had such an impact on the state and region. With Ray Christensen behind the mic telling us what we needed to know about the game, and Jules Perlt resonating from the public address system, Gopher football was at its best.

All those who listened to Ray Christenson for any or all of those 50 years and 500 games received a special reward.

***

The Gopher football announcing team is now made up of play-by-play man Dave Lee and color commentators Dave Mona and former Gopher running back Darrell Thompson. The three of them are terrific. Each has a unique style and provides great insight for each broadcast.

Dave Lee is noted for his work as the host of the WCCO morning news. Lee has received several broadcast awards, including the Associated Press' Minnesota play-by-play award five times, and is a multiple recipient of the National Association of Sports Broadcasters and Sportswriters' Minnesota Sportscaster of the Year Award.

Lee has great passion for Gopher football and is a huge promoter of Gopher sports and the University of Minnesota.

"The University is so special," says Lee, "and there are so many special people there. And there have been so many great players and great people."

It means so much to Lee to follow someone on the microphone like Ray Christensen.

"Ray was like being around a library," says Lee. "He did it all."

Dave Mona has had an incredible impact on the Minnesota sports scene through his Sunday radio broadcast of the *Sports Huddle* and his connection for many years to the University of Minnesota. With a 40-year association with Gopher sports, Mona brings a wealth of knowledge to the job. Mona has a solid background locally and regionally in the public relations industry. He and his wife Linda have donated countless hours to the University of Minnesota, and he is the past national president of the University of Minnesota Alumni Association. He was a key supporter of the TCF Bank Stadium and was most recently recognized by the Board of Regents as the 2008 recipient of the prestigious University of Minnesota Outstanding Achievement Award, an award his wife received a decade earlier.

"My connection to Gopher football goes back to 1954-1955 with my dad," says Mona. "It was all so special following the Gophers for all these years."

In his early days with the *Minnesota Daily*, Mona wrote a piece about the Gophers practicing some new strategy involving Bobby Bell and an unbalanced line, only to be called into Coach Warmath's office to discuss his article. It seems the coach wasn't too happy about anyone giving

The Gopher football announcing team—Darrell Thompson, Dave Lee and Dave Mona.

future opponents information about a Gopher practice session.

It never happened again, but Mona is proud to tell the story that Coach Warmath thought enough about what he had written to call him into his office to talk about it, even if he was upset about the content.

The third member of the Gophers' radio broadcast team is Darrell Thompson, one of the premier running backs to ever put on the maroon and gold uniform. He is the Gophers' all-time rushing leader and remains the only Minnesota player to rush for over 4,000 yards in his collegiate career. Thompson, highly recruited out of Rochester, Minnesota, scored a career 40 rushing touchdowns, had twenty-three 100-yard rushing games, and had a total of 5,109 all-purpose rushing and receiving yards in his career, the most ever by a Gopher player.

Thompson is very active in the community and is the Executive Director of the Bolder Options Program in Hennepin County, serving youth who are first-time offenders.

Thompson provides great insight to game listeners with his player experience and passion for Gopher football. His approach to the game is always interesting and entertaining. "I have been doing this for 12 years," he says, "and I really enjoy it. Working with Dave Lee and Dave Mona is great. And I also really enjoyed working with Ray Christensen. He is such a great person. I really take the time to do a lot of game preparation. I spent one season on the field but enjoy being up in the booth more, working beside Dave and Dave. I really enjoy the close connection that I have been able to keep with Gopher football."

Before and after the Golden Gopher broadcasts, Mike Grim hosts a pre- and post-game show that many fans enjoy. Grim, the voice of Gopher basketball, is from St. Louis, where he was the host of the nation's longest running sports talk program, the *Jeep Sports Open Line*. Grim was a lead afternoon sports anchor and did pre- and post-game shows in St. Louis for the Rams, Cardinals, Missouri Tigers and St. Louis Billikins. Grim's enthusiasm and broadcast expertise make him a natural to provide thoughtful game analysis.

***

The sounds of students and fans cheering, clapping, singing and encouraging the team at every Gopher game are perhaps the most recognizable to Gopher faithful.

Gopher games always include one of the most heralded fight songs ever played on a collegiate gridiron, The Minnesota Rouser. The history behind the Rouser goes back to 1909, when a contest was held by the *Minneapolis Tribune* and the *Minnesota Daily* for a fight song to replace "Hail Minnesota," which was felt to be too somber for its purpose.

The Minnesota Rouser was written by Floyd Hutsell, at the time the choir director of First Methodist Episcopal Church in Minneapolis. Today only the refrain is sung, although Hutsell's work originally included a verse as well. Hutsell titled his piece "Minnesota Hats Off to Thee," but it eventually became known as The Minnesota Rouser.

And there is a little irony to the contest story. It seems another songwriter by the name of William T. Purdy also wrote a song for the Minnesota contest. He titled his song "Minnesota Minnesota." At the closing moments of the contest, Purdy withdrew his song and decided to enter it into a similar contest at the University of Wisconsin. He renamed his entry "On Wisconsin."

The lyrics to The Minnesota Rouser:

Minnesota Hats off to thee! To thy colors true we shall ever be,

Firm and strong united are we.
Rah, rah, rah, for Ski-U-Mah
Rah! Rah! Rah! Rah!
Rah for the U of M.
M-I-N-N-E-S-O-T-A!
Minnesota, Minnesota!
Yeh, Gophers!

The phrase *Ski-U-Mah* was part of an early Minnesota cheer. While the song is being sung, Minnesota Gopher fans traditionally thrust their fist in the air during the spell-out, and twirl their index fingers during the yell. Before the Gopher football games when the Minnesota Football Marching Band comes across the field playing the Minnesota Rouser and the crowd stands in honor, it is a college football scene second to none.

Another song that fills the hearts of the Gopher faithful is "Hail! Minnesota." This song was originally called "Minnesota" and dates back to the early 1900s, when a group of students decided to honor their graduating class with a new song. In 1945, the Minnesota State Legislature approved it as the state song.

"Hail! Minnesota" was composed in 1904 by Truman Rickard and was performed for the very first time on May 28 on Class Day. The song's original second verse honored then University president Cyrus "Prexy" Northrop. Although humbled by the song's intention, Northrop indicated his preference for the song to honor the state and the school. Arthur Upson, editor of the *Minnesota Daily*, composed a new second verse. The song gained tremendous popularity over the next few years and began to be sung at football games after a touchdown. Although popular, the song's slow tempo did not seem appropriate for the atmosphere of a football game and was eventually replaced with the Minnesota Rouser.

It is traditional that the Minnesota Marching Band plays "Hail Minnesota" at the game's end, so fans who stay for the band's post-game performance can hear the song. The University version of the song is as follows:

Minnesota, Hail to thee!
Hail to Thee, our college dear!
Thy light shall ever be
A beacon bright and clear.

Thy sons and daughters true
Will proclaim Thee near and far.
They will guard thy fame and adore thy name;
Thou shalt be their Northern Star!

Like the stream that bends to sea,
Like the pine that seeks the blue;
Minnesota still for Thee
Thy sons are strong and true!
From the woods and waters fair,
From the prairies waving far.
At thy call they throng
With their shout and song;
Hailing Thee their Northern Star!

The sounds of Gopher football are perhaps best characterized by the University of Minnesota Football Marching Band. Founded in 1892 and first known as the University Cadet Band, its original membership numbered only 29. The first half time show was presented during the Gophers' 1910 football season. One of the formations used during that inaugural year was the "Block M" and this has become a symbol of the University of Minnesota.

The band has gone through many significant changes. The first major change in direction came when it merged with the Army to form the First Regiment of Minnesota Band in 1918. A Second Regiment of Minnesota Band was also in existence, but dissolved later that same year. After the war, all students who were involved in either one of the bands were invited back to join a separate University of Minnesota Band, which no longer used the word "Cadet' in its name.

Women eventually became band members, first entering the concert band in 1934. A Girls Band was formed in 1950, which became a Women's Division of the marching band, and remained for quite a few years until women became regular band members in 1972.

The Minnesota Marching Band has had the honor for many years of providing the support for the university athletic programs in an enthusiastic and disciplined manner, bringing about recognition and pride to the University both at home and on the road. Its representative role in support of the University and Gopher teams has always been an accomplishment worthy of the very highest esteem. The band performs at all football games and also performs at concerts and special events during the year. The marching band has had a total of 18 directors and 58 drum majors who had the distinct honor of leading one of the greatest marching bands in the nation.

All students have the opportunity to become a part of the marching band, registering for it just as if it were another class. There are no auditions except for the 30-member drum line. As many as 20 or more different collegiate majors are represented by band members, with students from virtually all colleges within the University's academic programs comprising the band.

Marching band begins with a a ten-day training session in late August. The band is led by Tim Diem, current Marching Band Director.

Gopher football head coach Tim Brewster recognizes the role of the band in preparing his Gophers for Saturday games. As the Gophers come off the practice field, the Marching Band is often set up in the giant field house, playing the Minnesota Rouser as the team heads to the locker room.

"Now listen closely here," says Brewster. "When you go through the band on the way to the locker room, I want each of you to stop right on the 50 yard line and show them how much you appreciate what they mean to us."

It is quite a sight to observe. The spirits come up, the aches drift away for the moment. The Gophers run onto the indoor practice facility field from outside, and the band is lined up on each side of the walkway. The players stop at the 50-yard line and cheer and clap for their band, recognizing the contribution the band makes to the team's success.

***

It is fitting to include someone else in this list of voices behind the Gophers. Although this character rarely speaks, his presence at games, cheering the team and exhorting the fans, is part of Gopher tradition. This legendary character is none other than Goldy Gopher.

Goldy Gopher is the mascot for the University of Minnesota sports teams associated with the Twin Cities campus and its Golden Gophers. A typical year finds Goldy Gopher at multiple public appearances as well as Gopher football and basketball games. In 2007, Goldy was voted a member of the Capital One All-American Mascot Team.

There are some interesting background facts concerning the beloved Goldy. The Gopher was originally based on a picture of a thirteen-lined ground squirrel. Though the gopher was the university's official mascot, the artist commissioned to draw the figure did not know what a gopher looked like. Thus the original Goldy looked very little like a gopher; in fact many thought Goldy's tail and buckteeth more closely resembled a beaver.

Over the years, Goldy's appearance changed. At one time, the mascot actually wore a freshman beanie, and by the 1950s the mascot, now called Goldy, wore clothes and played the drum.

In the 1960s and 1970s, Goldy looked more like a cartoon character and had an extensive athletic wardrobe. In the late 1970s and early 1980s, the mascot became more aggressive looking, but by the late 1980s Goldy took on the friendly look that we see today.

Goldy is there with the Gophers every Saturday, cheering the team, exciting the fans, working with the band and cheerleaders. The Football Marching Band had original responsibility for Goldy, with the supervision shifting to the athletic department in 1992.

The University of Minnesota Marching Band centennial book *Minnesota Hats Off to Thee*, published in 1992 by the University of Minnesota Band Alumni Society, notes that Minnesota's maroon and gold colors have long provided a symbol for the University of Minnesota. The colors were selected by Mrs. Augusta Norwood Smith, the grandniece of statesman Rufus Choate, who was an English instructor at the University of Minnesota between 1876 and 1880. There is no record of the exact date of the choosing of the colors, but it is believed to have been made during a time when Mrs. Smith was an instructor at the University.

Public address announcers, radio broadcasters, national television commentators, fans, the marching band, Goldy Gopher and the maroon and gold colors have been a part of football Saturdays, and have brought to the listeners and those in attendance something exceptional. Without them, Gopher football just wouldn't be the same.

6

LOVE AND PASSION FOR THE MAROON AND GOLD

Minnesota Golden Gopher football arrived in the 1880s as part of the University of Minnesota. During the run of great Rose Bowl teams in the early 60s, the Vikings and the Twins arrived in the Twin Cities and later the Timberwolves. The Minnesota North Stars came and went. And now the Wild are also here to capture the sports-minded public's attention.

But Gopher football is special to the Twin Cities. And who better to represent that celebrated tradition than Joel Maturi, athletic director for the University of Minnesota. Maturi is in his seventh year as the University's athletic director, and he is credited with turning the department into a model for all NCAA Division 1-A schools.

When Joel was hired in 2002 as the Director of Athletics, he became the first director to run both the men's and women's athletic departments at the University of Minnesota. He identified four major goals and has achieved them all in grand fashion. Maturi has merged the departments, balanced the budget, achieved broad-based success in athletics at the University, and brought the football team back to campus. Noteworthy is Joel's dedication, vision, passion and leadership.

Joel is from Chisholm, Minnesota, a proud product of one of the range cities. His love for the University of Minnesota Golden Gophers football team goes back to his childhood. In 1952, he attended his first Gopher football game, and although he remembers little of the final score or even who the Gophers were playing that day, he does remember the great atmosphere of football at the Brick House.

"I remember the people, the passion, the energy and the tremendous

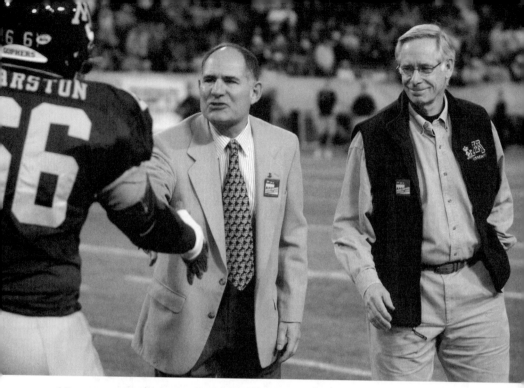

Minnesota Athletic Director Joel Maturi and President Robert Bruininks wish a Gopher player luck prior to kickoff.

excitement that was present at the game," recalls Maturi, lighting up as he recalls the experience. Maturi will see that excitement return in the fall of 2009 when the opening of TCF Bank Stadium completes the Gophers' "Greatest Comeback in Gopher History."

During Maturi's tenure as athletic director, he has led the school's 25 teams to both athletic and academic success. When Maturi arrived, the plan was to eliminate three of the programs due to grave budget concerns, but through Maturi's leadership and long-range planning the three sports survived, and the department is thriving.

Over the past seven years UM teams have earned four national championships, 24 Big Ten or WCHA regular season titles and five conference post-season titles. Maturi has also led the Gophers to a top 30 finish each year of the Directors Cup standings and in the 2007-08 years, he provided the oversight for three Big Ten titles, 16 teams participating in post-season competition and 225 academic all-conference selections and 19 academic all-district honors.

Maturi was instrumental in negotiating the $35 million naming rights sponsorship with TCF Bank, which is the largest corporate sponsorship in college football history. He also worked effectively with the 2006 state legislature to secure stadium funding.

Before his arrival as athletic director at the University, Joel Maturi was the Director of Athletics at Miami University (Ohio). From 1996-1998, he served as Director of Athletics at Denver University. Maturi worked in the athletic department at the University of Wisconsin from 1987-1996, serving as Associate Director of Athletics from 1992-1996. In 1993, he was named the Wisconsin Sports Person of the Year.

Before Maturi stepped into collegiate sports programs, he spent 19 years as a high school coach and administrator at Madison Edgewood High School. He coached football, basketball, baseball, and track and field, and led his teams to ten state tournaments. He was inducted into the Wisconsin Basketball Hall of Fame in 1992.

Joel Maturi received his B.A. in government from the University of Notre Dame in 1967 and earned a masters degree and certification for educational administration from the University of Wisconsin-Platteville in 1985. His record of success is outstanding, and he has brought the same fortitude and commitment to excellence to the University of Minnesota.

Maturi loves the tradition of Golden Gopher football. "I recall all of the great history of the past," says Maturi. "I remember the great Bronko Nagurski. I am proud to say I met him as a youngster. My dad knew him and they had a great connection."

When asked about the new stadium, Maturi lights up with pride for what it will mean to the University of Minnesota.

"The impact that the new TCF Bank Stadium will have is so significant. Football back on campus is going to be an experience, and the game day atmosphere is going to be really special," says Maturi.

"The stadium is not going to be for the students and alumni for 2009, 2010, 2011, or 2012, but rather for students, alumni, fans, the community, and the University for 100 years or more. And the stadium has not been built with flair, but it has been built with class, representing all of Minnesota. It is an extremely fan friendly place for all to enjoy," says Maturi.

Maturi was committed to bringing the University of Minnesota football team back to campus, and he did it by collaborating with many others to build the TCF Bank Stadium. He has a real connection to the his-

tory of Gopher football and a deep desire to have the Gophers start winning again.

"We have such great fans that have been so loyal for such a long time, and they have gone through so much disappointment," reflects Maturi. But the reality is he truly believes the Golden Gophers are on the right track.

Maturi is a strong believer in new Gopher head football Coach Tim Brewster.

"He is what I thought he was," says Maturi, when speaking of his decision to hire Brewster. "He is a tireless worker, a high-profile coach with high energy and a great recruiter. His enthusiasm will sell tickets, keep our great state athletes in state, and I just love the way he goes about everything."

Maturi's love for the University of Minnesota and particularly the student athletes is demonstrated by the number of athletic events that he attends as well as his communication with those involved in the athletic programs at the university. For example, every Sunday evening Maturi sends an email to each of his student athletes. On Sunday evening March 8, 2009, he sent the following message:

The thrill of victory and the agony of defeat! I have shared those words often because they are so true. Another great example is this past week. On Wednesday, men's basketball won a thriller against Wisconsin and on Saturday we lost a heartbreaker versus Michigan. As an Athletics Director I am close enough to our teams to witness the hard work that you put in during the year and the commitment made by your coaches and support staffs. What I have learned in my many years in this business is 'enjoy the journey.' There are no guarantees. The other team has probably worked hard and their staff's just as committed. In EVERY game there are 'breaks' that sometimes favor you and at other times go against you. When it is all said and done we leave the competition feeling good about our effort and the teammates we spent many hours with. I repeat—enjoy the journey! At this time of the year, our journey ends for some. As the winter season comes to an end some of our teams move on and others are eliminated. It is especially emotional for our seniors and understandably so. Thanks to all concluding their Gopher careers. This is the final week of classes

Maturi, a native of Chisholm, MN, attended his first Gopher football game in 1952.

before spring break; please 'take care of business' before you leave and return for the stretch run. Safe travel and some rest and relaxation for those not competing and good luck to those that are!   Joel

Maturi is a hard-driving worker whose heart rests in the right place. He cares deeply about the students and his staff and the University as a whole. The state, school, athletes, coaches, fans and all others he comes in contact with are fortunate to have him in his leadership role. He has made all who know him proud.

***

Working alongside Joel Maturi are his close associates, Tom Wistrcill and Marc Ryan. Each has an important role in Golden Gopher athletics and fills his role with pride.

Tom Wistrcill is the athletic director for external relations. Wistrcill comes from Wisconsin where he held the position of General Manager of Badger Sports Properties. He returned home, coming back to Minnesota where he started in 1993 as an assistant in the compliance office. He followed that position by serving as the Commissioner of the Northern Sun Intercollegiate Conference. He was also head of the 14-member Rocky Mountain Athletic Conference in Colorado Springs, Colorado, where he remained until 2000. He then worked four two years as vice-president of sales and marketing with VarsityOnline.com, and went on to become the General Manager of the St. Louis Qwest, a franchise in women's professional volleyball.

Marc Ryan listened to Gopher football when he was a youngster, captivated by legendary radio broadcaster Ray Christensen.

"I remember when former coach Butch Nash sat in our living room and recruited my brother to come to Minnesota. I will never forget it," recalls Ryan.

"I have been very fortunate to have worked for the athletic department for twenty years and met some great people and coaches. One of the greatest people I ever met was former Gopher Coach Jim Wacker. He was really extraordinary. He truly cherished every day of his life like it was a gift. Every time I left Jim's office, I had a spring in my step. He was so positive about everything. In Jim Wacker's world, there were very few down days," says Ryan. "I really liked working with all the other coaches as well, like John Gutekunst and Glen Mason."

Ryan is a graduate of Rosemount High School and started working at the University as the Assistant Sports Information Director in 1989. In 1994, he was promoted to the Sports Information Director, and in 1999 to the Assistant Athletic Director, under Dr. Mark Dienhart. In 2003, Joel Maturi named Ryan the Associate Athletic Director, with football one of his responsibilities.

Both Marc Ryan and Tom Wistrcill are great ambassadors for Gopher football, the athletic department and the University of Minnesota.

***

When talking passion and love for Minnesota Golden Gopher football, former Gopher quarterback Jim Reese must be part of the conversation. Jim was a quarterback and lettered in 1957-1958, and has great love for University of Minnesota football and Coach Murray Warmath. Jim has a great story to tell about the Michigan game of 1956 and two "guys" named Roger and Louie who turned the game around for the Gophers. Here is Jim's story.

THE LITTLE BROWN JUG - 1956
By Jim Reese

Veteran Minneapolis sportswriter Dick Cullum called it "one of the most glorious victories in the history of Minnesota football." After the Gophers had returned from Michigan to thousands of jubilant fans greeting their arrival at the airport, there was indeed no doubt as to the significance of that football game played on October 27, 1956.

Who could've thought that two guys named Roger and Louie would turn the game around in the Gophers' favor? Unseen in the program and unknown to all but the Minnesota football team, they would write one of the most unlikely chapters in the annals of this magnificent Midwest rivalry, the Minnesota-Michigan little Brown Jug game.

That same year, the University of Oklahoma, coached by former Minnesota All-American Bud Wilkinson, won the national championship. And it was from the Oklahoma playbook that Gopher coach Murray Warmath borrowed a page. Wilkinson was known for his split-T style of play, running play after play with such speed that opponents could never catch their breath and eventually just gave up.

Murray named his version of the Oklahoma offense "Roger and

Louie," and we practiced it incessantly before the big game. Disdaining a huddle, the Gophers ran a play and then hurriedly re-assembled a few yards behind the line of scrimmage, just long enough for the quarterback to whisper either Roger (right) or Louie (left) to his team, and off they raced to the line to quickly run another play, all from a balanced line and a full-house backfield, running either Roger or Louie.

The offense was tailor-made for a cunning quarterback, swift and agile linemen and rabbit-fast running backs. And that's

The original Little Brown Jug.

exactly what Minnesota had. So successful was this tactic that the Wolverines collapsed under the relentless number of plays being run at them. With magnificent Gopher quarterback Bobby Cox choosing the hole he wanted to run through (19 carries for 83 yards) or handing the ball off to a diving halfback or pitching to a trailing runner, the Gophers overcame a seven-point first half deficit to win 20-7.

But it wasn't the score that was significant as much as the way the game was played.

Playing before a partisan Michigan crowd of over 85,000 fans, the Gophers, with the second quarter one play old, had fallen behind 7-0 as a result of a Michigan 92-yard, sixteen-play scoring drive. The Gophers headed to the locker room hearing the cheers and jeers of their opponent's fans. That's when Murray called us all together and told us we were going to win by running the ball right down Michigan's throat with Roger and Louie.

Cox put the team on his shoulders and took the game over in the second half, directing clock-killing drives on three of four possessions by consistently running the ball. The three drives of 92, 28, and 47 yards all resulted in touchdowns, using up a total of 34 plays, all but one a run.

Michigan players were stunned by the swiftness of the Gopher attack, not only from the running game but from punt returns as well, a Warmath trademark. Bob Soltis and Pinky McNamara returned kicks into Michigan territory, returns begun by sleight-of-hand reverses from Dick Larson, both leading to scores. Conversely, so good was Gopher ball control and coverage that Minnesota punted but once all game, and that return by Michigan was for a meager nine yards. After their halftime lead had disappeared and Cox had taken over, the Wolverines appeared tired, disgruntled, dispirited and unable to cope with the onslaught of play after play after play being run at them. The Wolverines barely had a chance to line up on defense, so deft was Cox's play calling and the inspired no-huddle, time-consuming Gopher offense.

Thirty Golden Gophers played for Minnesota that day and to a man, over fifty years later, every one of us remembers fondly Roger and Louie.

Former *Minneapolis Tribune* writer Dick Cullum wrote about the great Gopher win in an article published October 27, 1956. It carried the headline:

GOPHERS ROCK MICHIGAN 20-7
Cox Flouts Wolverine Dignity to Pace Startling Comeback

Cullum's article read in part:

This was one of the most glorious victories in the history of Minnesota football.

The snarling Gophers came into Michigan's stadium as almost hopeless underdogs. They walked off the field the 20-7 victors. It was a magnificent come-from-behind effort in which they were out played throughout the first half and trailed 7-0. Then they outscored the Wolverines by 20-0 through a furiously played second half.

In this stretch of play they completely dominated the action and the major

*factor in the rout of the Wolverines, for rout it was indeed, was the swashbuck-
ling attitude and performance of Bobby Cox.*

*He took the field with a disdain for Michigan dignity and tradition and
made himself the boss of both teams, 84,639 spectators and the state of
Michigan.*

*When the Wolverines were waiting for him to put on his forward passing
stunts, he crossed them up by directing his attack mainly into the Michigan line
between the tackles. His ball handling was baffling to the opponents in which he
sneaked over center or ran keeper plays inside the tackles to keep the Minnesota
attack steadily on the move...A hard socking line, ball carriers who hit with
utter recklessness and field generalship which harassed the bewildered Michigan
team by the sizzling pace at which plays were called gave Minnesota an overwhelming superiority which became more and more evident with each
exchange...this rapid-fire attack directed mainly by Cox but brilliantly, also, by
Dick Larson, kept the Michigan defense continuously off balance....*

*It was a bold decision by which Coach Murray Warmath dared to come into
the home of the Wolverines and withhold his best stuff until the third quarter
while giving his opponent a good crack at the game in the first half...What a
transformation occurred when they came back for the second half, fresh, furious,
confident and full of tricks....*

*The Gophers completed four out of six passes attempted without an intercep-
tion, but the main point of the attack was that they did not use it when
Michigan was sure they would. Cox's willingness to grind it out on the ground
was a constant disturbing factor for the Michigan defense.*

The *Minneapolis Tribune* ran the following box score:

Michigan (7)
Left Ends - Kramer, Prahst
Left Tackles - Orwig, Heynen, Davies
Left Guards - Hill, Faul, Berger
Centers - Rotunno, Snider
Right Guards - Nyren, Corona
Right Tackles - Sigman, Marciniak
Right Ends - Maentz, Brooks, Johnson
Quarterbacks - Van Pelt, Maddock
Left Halfbacks - Pace, Ptacek
Right Halfbacks - Barr, Shannon, Shatusky
Fullbacks - Herrstein, Byers

Minnesota (20)
Left Ends - Jelacic, Gehring, Juhl
Left Tackles - Youso, Buckingham
Left Guards - Burkholder, Gerths, Kleber
Centers - Maas, Svendsen, Jukich
Right Guards - Barrington, Rasmussen, Wallin
Right Tackles - Hobart, Herbold
Right Ends - Fairchild, Schmidt, K. Schultz
Quarterbacks - Cox, Larson, Reese
Left Halfbacks - McNamara, Soltis, Bombardier
Right Halfbacks - Schultz, Lindholm, Chorske
Fullbacks - Tuszka, Blakley
Michigan Scoring: Touchdown - Barr (16 yard run), conversion-
   Kramer
Minnesota Scoring: Touchdowns - Schultz (30 yard run), Cox -2
   (3 and 7 yard plunges)
Conversions - Bombardier, Rasmussen."

The *Minneapolis Tribune* also ran an article from Russell Bull, *Tribune* photographer, that read in part:

When the Gophers returned home from Michigan they were greeted by the largest crowd of football fans ever assembled at Wold Chamberlain airport. Every foot of space was taken, with hundreds of fans unable to get into the airport terminal. When the players stepped out of the plane, loud cheers went up from the fans that jammed the observation deck...

***

Jim Reese loved playing for Murray Warmath and has many fond memories of the legendary Gopher football coach.

"Murray had a warm and gracious smile and was very sure of himself, a very confident man," says Reese.

"Some years ago there was reunion of some of his original players from the 50s. During a speech he was giving, Murray told all the guys that he apologized if he had ever done anything to hurt anyone's feelings in his dealings with them as their coach. He said he was sorry and that he never meant to hurt anyone. Based on my observations of the man, he will never have any reason to apologize to players, fans, the

University or opponents for anything he ever did," said Reese.

"After a successful 1954 season of 7-2, he followed up with a 3-6 record in 1955, and a 6-2-1 record in 1956, which resulted in the Gophers being the 1957 pre-season pick to be ranked number 1 in the country. After a 3-0 start, things went into a tailspin and from that time until the end of the 1959 season, Murray's record was 4-19. People in the Twin Cities were throwing garbage on his lawn and wanting to ride him out of town on a rail," recalls Reese.

"I spent an awful lot of time with him as a player and coach during those tough times, and never once did I see him lose his temper, treat anyone unfairly, or be anything other than a great role model for young men. Probably the lowest point I can remember was at Iowa in 1959, seeing from my vantage point in the press box a vanquished Murray, a 33-0 loser, shaking hands with the opposing coach, walking across the field to the distant locker room, his familiar checkered overcoat hanging on his weary shoulders, very alone it seemed. And I remember how he recovered from that low point in his coaching life to come back the very next year and win the Big Ten title and the national championship. He never, ever gave up! That will always be the legacy of Murray Warmath."

***

One of the great Gopher players of all time was Mike Wright. Wright played tackle at Minnesota during some lean years, played pro football in Canada, and later became an attorney and CEO of Super Value Stores in the Twin Cities. Wright was a superb lineman and although he was on Gopher teams in the late 1950s that managed only 7 wins and 20 losses, he cherishes every minute that he was connected to the Golden Gophers.

Mike Wright has always had high regard for Coach Murray Warmath and saw him handle some of the toughest times in Gopher football history. With a season of disappointment in 1957, after such high hopes had been deflated, and then to follow with only three victories the next two seasons, he experienced what few Gophers have gone through. He never had the enjoyment of the great winning seasons that followed, but

Former head coach Murray Warmath.

it doesn't seem to matter to Wright when he talks of his great regard for the University of Minnesota and the Gopher football program.

Coach Warmath was very special to Mike Wright. Wright was the team captain in 1959, an Academic All-American, and one of the team leaders. Like Jim Reese, one of Wright's great memories is of the way Warmath handled the tough years as head coach for the Gophers. Wright speaks from the heart when he talks of Coach Warmath saying, "If the guys didn't quit, why would I quit," and what that sentiment meant to the team.

He also talks of the great inner strength of Murray Warmath.

"He never seemed to waiver in what he believed in," says Wright. "I have the utmost respect, love and admiration for him. He had a tough mental philosophy that if the team wasn't winning, then maybe they weren't working hard enough so he worked us very hard. I learned a lot about life from Coach Warmath," recalls Wright. "There are a lot of people facing the same things that the coach faced and would have cracked under the pressure. Coach Warmath did not."

Coach Warmath guided Mike Wright through one of the toughest decisions in his life regarding going to law school.

"He always gave us good advice and knew law school was the right choice for me, and helped me to do both football and school," says Wright.

Mike Wright recalls the great difficulty of the 1959 season for the coach and the team. He proudly recalls a letter that he received from Mrs. Warmath a week after the hard-fought Purdue loss in 1959, speaking of the coach and how much it meant to him that the team, even in the height of adversity, never quit. The letter read in part:

Dear Mike,

I want to tell you how wonderful I think you are and the whole team is...he just felt like he has lost so much face . . . you fellows did the job and what a terrific game it was though I'm sure you didn't feel like playing the way you did. I have never seen anybody as happy as Murray was and the other coaches. Thank you again Mike.

Sincerely,

Mrs. M. Warmath.

Though these players experienced the frustration and disappointment of losing, they never gave up and the coach never gave up. And those that played during those times remember how their coach taught them to hold their heads high.

Warmath has often been credited with breaking the color barrier by heavily recruiting black athletes to come to northern schools. And he did it in a professional and sensitive manner. Coach Warmath had no issue with the color of a man's skin; his only concern rested with whether he could play football, and he treated everyone the same. He always went out of his way to assist the players in what must have been an uncomfortable transition for them. He leaned on players like Mike Wright to be the team leaders.

"Work hard, play hard and set a good example," Warmath told Wright when he was elected team captain. And the coach's expectations have never been forgotten.

Warmath set the example for working hard and carrying on the Minnesota winning tradition. When Mike Wright played in Canada, he played for Bud Grant, who was a Gopher legend and head coach of the Vikings. Wright recalls how there have only been a few coaches who could command complete attention of a crowd of people when they spoke: Bear Bryant at Alabama, Woody Hayes at Ohio State, Bud Grant and Murray Warmath.

"When they spoke, people listened," says Wright.

Sometime around 1962-63, the *Minneapolis Tribune* ran an article before a game against Purdue.

The last time Murray Warmath visited Purdue with the Minnesota squad in 1959, he was debating his future at the University as the head football coach. The Gophers were having a rough year with only two victories. After a 33-0 loss to Iowa, Warmath was giving some consideration to resigning. 'The only fellows in the room who are sure of their future are the seniors on this team,' Warmath told the Minnesota squad, the Thursday afternoon before the 1959 Purdue game.

That same week the Gopher mentor had called up his assistant coaches and informed them he wouldn't stand in their way and wouldn't blame them if they decided to leave for greener pastures. The Gophers lost that game to Purdue 29-23, but played well enough that Warmath had a change of heart, and decided to stick out his four-year contract at Minnesota.

Four years later, conditions are a lot different after three great winning sea-

sons in 1960, 1961 and in 1962. Warmath is a full professor at the University and has won statewide support. The Gophers have won only one Big Ten game this season, but there haven't been any complaints and there shouldn't be after the three-year record Warmath and his staff have compiled.

***

The 1960 team that went on to win the national championship and the great Gopher teams that followed comprised a special group of players. Some had been a part of the losing 1958-1959 seasons.

"I don't think anyone realized how good Sandy Stephens, Bobby Bell and Carl Eller were going to be. They were exceptional players and great team leaders," said Dick Larson, Gopher quarterback from 1955-1957 and former assistant coach.

"Just take a look at those rosters during those years and count the number of players that went on to play professional football, and it gives an indication of how good the players were. And they were not only great players but they were special people, too."

"When I was a kid, I used to scramble to find a radio to listen to Gopher football on Saturday afternoons," said Larson. "It was a special time. I first met Murray Warmath at a track meet at Memorial Stadium when I was in high school," recalls Larson. "I didn't have a father and he became like a father figure to me. He was so much in charge of everything. He was everywhere and had a real presence about him. I was with Coach Warmath all the time at quarterback meetings and on the field. He was a great coach to play for. I have never had more fun playing the game of football," says Larson.

Dick Larson was an outstanding player for the Minnesota Gophers and has such tremendous pride in his role as a member of the Gophers teams. In 1957, Dick Larson was named the team's Most Valuable Player.

***

When we look back at Minnesota Gopher football through the years, there may be no one more involved in the every day workings of the team than Dick Mattson, the equipment manager for several decades. Mattson is from Benson, Minnesota, and became a student manager for football in 1961. No one lived, breathed and loved Gopher football more than Dick Mattson. He was always there. He always knew what was

The dynamic Sandy Stephens.

going on and he deeply cared about people and the University. Mattson treated everyone the same. It didn't matter if a player was an All-American or a back-up who never got on the field. They were all Gopher football players and he respected everyone for that reason.

When Mattson speaks about Gopher football, one of the first names he brings up is George "Butch" Nash. Nash is a true Gopher football legend. It seemed as though he was a part of the program forever. Nash played for Minnesota from 1936-1938; he was an end on Bernie Bierman's national championship squad of 1936 and the Big Ten championship teams of 1937 and 1938. Nash worked as an assistant coach with the Gophers from 1947 to 1991, totaling 44 years!

During his playing days at Minnesota, Nash was also a guard on the Gopher basketball team. Before getting into the college coaching ranks at the University of Minnesota, Nash was a successful high school coach at Anoka and Winona, leading Winona to the Big Nine championship in 1941.

Since 1984, the Gopher football team has honored Nash by establishing the Butch Nash Award, given annually to the Gopher football player who best demonstrates competitiveness on the football field and in academics.

Nash's pride in Gopher football was something to behold. He wanted to win more than anything, and he often demonstrated his passion to

Gopher squads.

In 1977, a heavily favored Michigan team came into Memorial Stadium set to crush the Gophers and went down to defeat in one of the great Gopher upset wins of all time. In 1986, the Minnesota squad, again monumental underdogs, traveled to Ann Arbor to face the Wolverines. The evening before the game, Coach John Gutekunst's players watched film of the great Minnesota victory over Michigan in 1977. After seeing the films, Nash, a volunteer assistant at the time, addressed the team with an inspirational speech. Anthony Burke, an offensive tackle, said after Nash's speech the Gopher squad was ready to take the field that night! Nash talked of the Gophers leaving their blood and skin right there on the field in that 1977 win and showed his desire for the Gophers to do the same the next day. And with a late field goal to clinch the victory, that's what the Gophers did.

Butch Nash died in 2005 at the age of 89, with a heart full of maroon and gold and memories of the great wins over Michigan resting next to his soul.

"I remember them all," said Dick Mattson, "and there were some great ones, players and coaches. Cal Stoll was a great coach, he had many successful players, and he really allowed his coaches to do their jobs. Bob Woodenhoffer and Dick Mosely, two assistant coaches, what great guys they were, and how they worked with the kids was so incredible," recalls Mattson. "And Murray Warmath, I loved Murray!"

"One of the best I have ever seen play here was Bobby Bell. He had such a great attitude and was such a phenomenal player. I remember the game in 1961 when he cracked his ribs in the first half of the game, got taped up and went out to play in the second half after his father said to him, 'I didn't drive 2000 miles to see you sit on the bench.' He was so talented and always so joyful," said Mattson. "I truly think he may have had the greatest attitude of any player to play at Minnesota. He could have played any position on the team, and I have seen all the great ones here over many years. Bobby just took care of everyone and he had such tremendous physical ability."

"And there were so many others," recalls Mattson. "I loved Tony Dungy and had such respect for him as a player and as a person. Those

Gopher football legend George "Butch" Nash.

like Chuck Killian, Paul Faust were such great captains and great people, and the others like Gordy Condo and Tom Sakal, great players and great characters, great Gophers."

"The Michigan game in 1986 was a wonderful memory for me," recalled Mattson. "After the game, we hugged and we cried and quarter-back Rickie Foggie said, 'This one is for Butch and Matts!' It was a great day!"

Dick Mattson is special, and all those who know him will never forget all he did for Gopher football.

***

Dick Mattson mentioned former Gopher assistant Dick Mosely and how he excelled at working with players. Dick Mosely was with the Gophers during the great 1977 upset win over Michigan. At half time, Mosely gave an inspiring half time talk:

Haven't got one adjustment to give you. You are playing super. It was one of the greatest halves...did you hear my words? It was one of the greatest halves we as coaches ever had the privilege of being a part of. You are on the brink of history! Praise God you can come back and do just what you can do; no more. And they will write stories about you all your life!!

Now...Michigan is right over there gathering themselves together. They're the number one team in the United States of America. Now let me tell you something. They are not going to abandon their game plan. They are going to come back with tightened up belts. Their chinstraps are going to be tight. They're going to have poise and they're going to come right at you. They are not going to panic because this game is in balance. They know it...and you know it. But it ain't going to be enough...if you want it. They haven't got enough in their arsenal. We'll play the game plan like we had it. Men, you've got 13 solid points on the board for you.

What did we tell you? They're playing the wrong team at the wrong time at the wrong place...and they're half way out of gas. Now have we got enough to finish them off? It's your game men.

October 22, 1977
Final Score: Minnesota 16 Michigan 0.

"I loved coaching with Cal Stoll," said Dick Mosely. "He was a truly loyal person and deeply cared for people. He had a real presence about him and really cared for the players. I remember when one of our guys became seriously ill, Cal Stoll was there with him everyday. He was a great person. I can't think of anyone I had more respect for than Cal Stoll. He was so genuine in every respect."

"I also had great respect for Butch Nash who loved the Gophers so much. He used to always say that Bobby Bell was the greatest Gopher ever, without a moment's hesitation. He was such a great representative of the Gophers. He cared so much and if there was ever a true Gopher to the end and to praise, it would be Butch Nash," said Mosely.

"And how can you not speak of Dick Mattson when you talk Gopher football. He was such an inspiration to the players and to the coaching staff as well. He was really one of the guys. I really loved my time in Minnesota," recalls Mosely. "It was a very memorable time in my life."

***

Two-time All-American Bob Stein.

"It was really a big deal for me to play football at the University of Minnesota," says Bob Stein, two-time All-American, Academic All-American, three time All-Big Ten player and great defensive end for the Gophers.

"I was very frustrated that my dad never saw me play at Minnesota. When he died, Coach Warmath was just great to my family and me. He came to the funeral and lifted my spirits by saying to me that he thought I was going to make it big with the

Gophers. He was a very kind man," recalls Stein.

Stein remains appreciative that he was able to follow legends at Minnesota like Bobby Bell, who he later played with as a member of the Kansas City Chiefs.

"Bell was really something," recalls Stein. "He was the best athlete I ever saw. He was just incredible physically. I think he had a 28" waist and could do anything on the field. He could throw a football farther than our punter could kick the ball or our quarterback could throw the ball. The first time he lifted a weight, he lifted 300 pounds. He could catch a fly right out of the air. He was a smart, tough football player, and I loved being around him," said Stein.

One of the things that Stein likes to mention when talking about Coach Murray Warmath are the Warmath "game maxims," and Stein doesn't hesitate to recite them verbatim:

"The team that makes the fewest mistakes wins the game. Play for and make the breaks and when one comes your way—SCORE. If at first the game — or the breaks — go against you, don't let up...put on more steam. Protect our kickers, our quarterback, our lead and our ball game. Ball, "Oskie," cover, block, cut and slice, pursue and gang tackle....for this is the WINNING EDGE. Press the kicking game. Here is where the breaks are made. Carry the fight to our opponent and keep it there for 60 minutes."

That was the way Coach Warmath thought about winning football games. And although over 40 years have passed since Bob Stein played for his coach, he still remembers the game maxims. He keeps them handy because he's found they also apply to life.

***

Chuck Killian was the captain of the Golden Gophers in 1966. Killian was an outstanding center and is a class person. The Gopher tradition and the University of Minnesota mean a great deal to Killian, and he has been an active fundraiser for the new TCF Bank Stadium. He wants to see the great tradition of the past rekindled. He believes that with the opening of the new stadium and the enthusiasm and commitment of Coach Tim Brewster, the Gophers have a good chance of returning to their winning tradition.

Chuck recalls his fondness for Murray Warmath, Butch Nash and coaches like Bob Bossons, Jerry Annis, and so many others who helped bring the Gophers to national prominence in the early 1960s.

"You always knew where you stood with Coach Warmath," says Killian. "He was always very direct with you. When I was elected captain of the 1966 team, I was expected to be the team leader and I took the responsibility very seriously. It was a great honor. And I loved to be around Coach Bob Bossons also. He was a great defensive coach. He was a wonderful guy and a fabulous football coach."

***

Joe Pung was another outstanding Gopher football player and captained the 1964 Gophers.

"I was elected captain of the 1964 Gophers following a team meeting after the 1963 season. It was a tremendous responsibility and a great honor," says Pung.

Pung has some wonderful memories of the great Gopher teams that he was a part of in the early 1960s. However, he also has some less-than-positive memories.

He recalls the infamous Wisconsin game at Madison that ended not with a Badger lucky break or miracle play but with one of the worst calls by an official in Gopher history. The fateful day is now often referred to as "The Day the Jesse James Gang Rode into Madison Disguised as Game Officials."

The final outcome on November 24, 1962, had the Badgers prevailing over the Gophers by a score of 14-9. There will always be calls that upset coaches, players and fans. Most are remembered for a while but are soon forgotten. This official's decision, however, has lived on for some four and a half decades.

The Gophers and Badgers came into the game tied for first place in the Big Ten. The game was played at Camp Randall before a record crowd of 65,514 spectators. It had been an incredibly hard fought contest, with both teams showing their prowess on the field, evidence of their claim to the Big Ten championship. Late in the fourth quarter with the Gophers leading 9-7, Wisconsin took over possession on their own 20-yard line following a Gopher punt. The Badgers drove the ball to the Gopher 43 yard line with 2:30 left in the game. The next play provided the impetus for disaster.

Wisconsin quarterback Ron VanderKelen dropped back to pass to end Pat Richter. Gopher All-American Bobby Bell crashed through the line and got to VanderKelen as he tried to make the pass. The ball spun off VanderKellen's finger tips and fluttered into the grasp of Gopher linebacker Jack Perkovich as Bell drove the signal caller into the turf.

Perkovich returned the interception to the Gopher 42 yard-line, and the game was essentially over. Minnesota had regained possession and all but won the game and the Big Ten championship.

But just as the Gopher fans, players and coaches began to celebrate, an official's decision changed the course of the game. Lying on the ground just behind the fallen quarterback and the great Gopher All-American was an official's yellow flag. Referee Bob Jones had called a roughing the passer penalty on Bobby Bell, a fifteen-yard march off against the Gophers. Wisconsin was going to keep possession of the ball, the interception would be nullified and the Big Ten crown shifted from the Twin Cities to Madison in an instant.

The outrage over the call didn't end with the Gopher loyal in attendance or all those glued to their radios. And it didn't end with the players or the Gopher assistant coaches. Head coach Murray Warmath was infuriated.

In the midst of the shock and dismay, another official was walking down the sideline near the Gopher bench and Warmath reached out and tugged at his sleeve to get his attention, asking why the penalty was called against Bell. The official immediately hollered at Warmath that he was out of line by touching him and threw another penalty flag for unsportsmanlike conduct on the part of the Gopher coach, another fifteen-yard penalty.

The thirty yards of penalties against Minnesota gave Wisconsin the ball at the Gopher 13 yard-line. The Badgers scored shortly thereafter and kicked the point after, taking a 14-9 lead. The Gophers made several furious attempts to score at the end of the game, but to no avail.

It was over. It seemed surreal. How could this have happened? One of the greatest Gopher football teams ever had lost a game and the Big Ten championship, not because of their play but because of an official's call.

An outraged Murray Warmath was escorted from the field by Athletic Director Ike Armstrong and Big Ten Commissioner Bill Reed. At the game's conclusion, the officials locked themselves in the locker room,

Warmath had to be escorted from the field following the roughing the passer penalty against Bobby Bell towards the end of the 1962 Wisconsin-Minnesota game.

quashing attempts by several Gopher players, led by Carl Eller, to get to them.

Warmath, however, would not be stopped in his attempt to confront the "James Gang." He stayed outside the officials' locker room and when the door opened to let someone in, Warmath charged through the door, grabbing one official along the way and confronting the rest of them. They quietly listened to Warmath's critique of their on-field work. Warmath let them have it with both barrels, telling them that they had stolen the Big Ten championship from Minnesota. He told them they had taken it away from the finest group of young men he had ever known, and they would never be forgiven for their unfairness and incompetence. Warmath chose to keep this confrontation confidential, only talking about it after many years had passed.

Bell never believed that he had roughed up the Wisconsin quarterback. He felt that he had hit VanderKelen long before he released the football and that it wasn't even close to being a penalty. A picture of Bobby Bell at an introduction ceremony before the Army-Navy game in

1962 shows Bell shaking hands with President John F. Kennedy as the year's All-Americans were being honored. As President Kennedy shook Bell's hand, he remarked about the penalty called against Bell in the Wisconsin game. Even the President of the United States had not forgotten what happened to the Golden Gophers "The Day the Jesse James Gang Rode into Madison."

"The game was stolen from us," recalls Pung. "I will never forget it."

The Gophers finished 6-2-1 that year and the game cost them a potential third consecutive trip to the Rose Bowl. The 1962 Gopher team was one of the best ever, only to lose its final game on such a sour note.

There is an old joke told about the game that does have some significance.

It seems that three athletes who had died were standing at the Pearly Gates. Each was waiting for his admission interview with Saint Peter.

The first athlete told Saint Peter that he had been a professional baseball player for 20 years, had toiled in the minor leagues for half of his career, but when eventually reaching the big leagues, lost many more games than he won. Saint Peter looked him in the eye and said, "Well, you had a nice two-decade career playing baseball and even though you were not a great star, it seems that you had a pretty good life. I think you need to spend a little time in Purgatory to experience some of the real toughness in life before you will be allowed through the Pearly Gates."

The second athlete arrived and said that he had played professional basketball for ten years and never started a game. He went on to say that his team never won a championship and that he was traded several times, having to uproot his family and move to new cities. Saint Peter said, "Well son, professional basketball has given you a good salary, a good life. I think we will have you spend some time below, experiencing some of the real perils in life before we will admit you above."

The third athlete met Saint Peter at the admission gates and said, "I played on the Minnesota Golden Gopher football team that lost to Wisconsin at Madison in 1962 and...." Saint Peter stopped the man and said, "Come right in, son. You have been through hell already!"

Joe Pung recalls how hard Coach Warmath used to work the squad in practices and said, "Murray almost killed us in practice. Our best competition seemed to always be against each other. And I remember being on the field with the great Bobby Bell as a freshman. I used to watch how he would just toy with us. He was absolutely unbelievable! Bobby was so quick and when you were lined up as linebacker behind him, he just made you look so good. He had such a great attitude also," recalls Pung.

"Another one of the great ones that I played with was Carl Eller. He was so big and so strong, and he had such great speed. We had a speedy halfback named Billy Crockett at the time and I saw Carl almost outrun him in a race. He was such a great athlete. It was a great experience playing for the Gophers. Coach Warmath taught me so much, things that I have used throughout my life," says Pung.

7

THE CAPTAINS

A great number of Gopher football players have worn the maroon and gold colors since 1882, but only 183 have been named captain. Only 15 were named captain twice.

Leaders of the maroon and gold, men of integrity, passion, pride, honor, commitment, courage and love for the university sums up the men to have shared the honor of serving as captain of the Golden Gophers.

Gopher captains are the commanders, the directors, the ringleaders and the team representatives on and off the field. They are looked up to by the players, the coaches and the fans. Some squads have chosen only one captain to lead; others have chosen more to represent them. But each has been chosen for the honor and has lived it to the fullest.

CAPTAINS OF THE GOLDEN GOPHERS

1882	A.J. Baldwin, RB
1883	John W. Williams, C
1884	No Captain
1885	Howard T. Abbott, QB
1886	Howard T. Abbott, QB
1887	Alfred Pillsbury, QB
1888	B.E. Trask, LE
1889	Alfred Pillsbury, QB
1890	Horace C. Robinson, C
1891	William C. Leary, HB
1892	William C. Leary, HB
1893	James Madigan, C
1894	Everhart Harding, RG
1895	August T. Larson, LG
1896	John M. Harrison, LE

1897	John M. Harrison, LE
1898	George E. Cole, QB
1899	Buzz Schandrett, RE
1900	L.A. "Bert" Page, C
1901	Warren Knowlton, FB
1902	John Flynn, LG
1903	Edward Rogers, LE
1904	Moses Strathern, C
1905	Earl Current, FB
1906	Earl Current, FB
1907	John Schuknecht, RH
1908	Ney Dunn, captain elect (died before the season) Orren Stafford, FB

1903 captain Ed Rogers

1909	John McGovern, QB
1910	Lisle Johnston, FB
1911	Earl Pickering, FB
1912	Paul Tobin, FB
1913	Donald Aldworth RE
1914	Boles Rosenthal, C
1915	Bernie Bierman LH
1916	Bert Baston
1917	George Hauser
1918	Norman Kingsley, FB
1919	Ernest Lampi, RH
1920	Neil Arnston, QB
1921	Larry Teberg, LT
1922	Oliver Aas, C
1923	Earl Martineau, QB
1924	Ted Cox, RT
1925	Herman Ascher, RH
1926	Roger Wheeler, RE
1927	Herb Joesting, FB
1928	George Gibson, LG
1929	Game Captains
1930	Win Brockmeyer, RH
1931	Clarence Munn, LG

1916 captain Bert Baston

1932 Walter Hass, QB

1933 Roy Oen, C

1934 Francis "Pug" Lund, HB

1935 Glen Seidel, QB

1936 Julius Alphonse, HB

1937 Ray King, RE

1938 Francis Twedell, RG

1939 Win Pederson, LT

1940 Bob Bjorklund, C
     Bill Johnson, E

1941 Bruce Smith, LH

1942 Dick Wildung, RT

1943 Paul Mitchell, T
     Clifford Anderson, E

1944 Game Captains

1945 Game Captains

1946 Robert Sandberg, QB

1947 Steve Silianoff, C

1948 Warren Beson, C

1949 Howard Brennan, C
     Clayton Tonnemaker, C

1950 Dave Skrien, FB

1951 Wayne Robinson, C

1952 Richard Anderson, G

1953 Paul Giel, HB

1954 Bob McNamara, HB

1955 Mike Falls, C

1956 Dean Maas, C

1957 Jon Jelacic, E

1958 Mike Svendsen, C

1959 Mike Wright, T

1960 Greg Larson, C

1961 John Mulvena, G

1962 Dick Enga, C

1963 Milt Sunde, T

1964 Joe Pung, C

1965 Paul Faust, G

1966	Chuck Killian, C
1967	Tom Sakal, RH
1968	Noel Jenke, LB
1969	Jim Carter, FB
1970	Jeff Wright, DHB
1971	Bill Light, LB
1972	Bob Morgan, QB
1973	Mike Steidl, MLB
1974	Ollie Bakken, LB
	Jeff Selleck, C
1975	Keith Simons, DT
1976	Tony Dungy, QB
1977	Steve Midboe, DT
1978	Stan Systma, DE
1979	Alan Blanshan, DT
	Glenn Bourquin, TE
	Mark Carlson, QB
1980	Marion Barber, TB
1981	Ken Dallafior, OT
1982	Ed Olson, C
1983	Randy Rasmussen, C
1984	Mark Vonderhaar, OT
1985	John Lilleberg, OG
	Peter Najarian, LB
1986	Mark Dusabek, LB
	Ray Hitchcock, C
	Norries Wilson, OT
1987	Ricky Foggie, QB
1988	Jason Bruce, FL
	Chuck McCree, CB
	Brian Williams, C
1989	Darrell Thompson, RB
	Mac Stephens, LB
1990	Mike Sunvold, DT
	Frank Jackson, FS
1991	Sean Lumpkin, DB
	Pat Evans, TE

1992 Keith Ballard, OL
Andre Davis, LB
Marquel Fleetwood, QB
Ted Harrison, OL

1993 Dennis Cappella, DL
Antonio Carter, RB
Russ Heath, LB
Robert Rogers, OL

1994 Chris Darkins, RB
Ed Hawthorne, DL

1995 Justin Conzemius, DB
Chris Darkins, RB
Todd Jesewitz, OL
Craig Sauter, QB

1996 Gann Brooks, OL
Jerome Davis, DL
Ben Langford, LB
Cory Sauter, QB

1997 Tutu Atwell, WR
Crawford Jordan, DB
Cory Sauter, QB
Parc Williams, LB

1998 Troy Duer, OT
Antoine Richard, DT
Parc Williams, LB

1999 Tyrone Carter, SS
Billy Cockerham, QB
Ben Hamilton, C

2000 Ben Hamilton, C
Sean Hoffman, LB
Karon Riley, DE

2001 Jack Brewer, FS
Derek Burns, C
Jimmy Henry, LB
Ron Johnson, WR

2002 Asad Abdul-Khaliq, QB
Michael Lehan, CB

1999 captain Tyrone Carter

128

2008 captains Eric Decker (right) and Adam Weber (left).

2003   Asad Abdul-Khaliq, QB
        Dan Kwapinski, DT
        Ben Utecht, TE
        Eli Ward, FS
2004   Greg Eslinger, C
        Justin Fraley, FS
        Rian Melander, OT
        Darrell Reid, DE
2005   Greg Eslinger, C
        Anthony Montgomery, DT
        John Pawielski, FS
        Mark Setterstrom, OG
2006   Mike Sherels, LB
        Matt Spaeth, TE
2007   Tony Brinkhaus, C
        Amir Pinnix, RB
        Mike Sherels, LB
        John Shevlin, LB
        Steve Shidell, OT
        Willie VanDeSteeg, DE
2008   Steve Davis, LB
        Eric Decker, WR
        Willie VanDeSteeg, DE
        Adam Weber, QB

"The captain is the person on the football team that the coach can rely on and depend on," says George Adzick, Director of the "M" Club. "It is an American tradition. The honor is representative of a team's iconic athletes who are the feature of a team and all the traditions of the past."

The captains of the Minnesota Gophers are not only endowed with great athletic ability but magnificent character and leadership. When one takes a close look at the past Gopher football captains, they jump out with respect to great athletic achievement. Twenty-two of the captains have been honored as All-Americans and nine are members of the College Football Hall of Fame.

They are the "front and center" of a football team. The other players look upon them as leaders and follow their example. Gopher head football coach Tim Brewster was a captain and he has a "Captain's Wall" outside of his office, signifying the importance of the honor to the team. Brewster depends on his captains on and off the field, and expects them to be responsible for captain's meetings and other important on-field functions.

"I look at our captains for leadership," says Brewster.

And there is no question that Brewster understands the importance of the role.

Captain — an honor bestowed upon a chosen few.

8

GOLDEN GOPHER COACHES

He was a football legend, and he used to walk onto the Northrop practice field in the fall wearing an old tan storm coat with an off white fur collar. It was always turned up. His white hair glistened and he looked tired: too many pressures, too many big games, and a lot of championships.

Bernie Bierman

A hush would come over the field when he first entered, and someone would ask, "What's going on?" Before long, someone else would quietly say, "Look over there, it's the Old Grey Eagle, Bernie Bierman."

He was there, watching football practice, perhaps longing for the days when he coached the Golden Gophers or perhaps just glad to have it all behind him. His history with the Gophers included winning five national championships. He was Bernie Bierman and he was bigger than life, one of the most successful coaches in the history of college football.

There have been 30 head

football coaches for the Minnesota Golden Gophers. It is an unusual history, with many of the early gridiron giants taking on the role for a one-year period. In fact, there were 13 coaches who coached for just one year, some of whom even shared the role with others during the season.

On the opposite end of the spectrum was Coach Henry Williams who lead the maroon and gold for 22 years, followed by Murray Warmath for 18 years and Bernie Bierman for 16 years. The three were the men in charge for 56 Gopher football seasons.

The Minnesota Gophers' inaugural football season was in 1882, and the team did not have a head football coach. The first Gopher game was played at the Minnesota State Fairgrounds in September, 1882. The game actually followed a scheduled track meet between Minnesota, Hamline University and Carleton College.

Carleton didn't show up for the meet, and after the Minnesota/Hamline contest concluded, the University of Minnesota athletes played Hamline in a football game. The Gophers won 4-0 and it was recorded as the first football game ever played. A few weeks later the teams had a rematch, won by Hamline. The Gophers' first football game was a mere afterthought following a track meet.

***

The first head football coach for the University of Minnesota was Tom Peebles, assigned to coach in 1883. Peebles was hired by the University of Minnesota to teach philosophy and because he had a football background at Princeton, he coached the football team. There were only three games played that season and Peebles' squad finished with a 1-2 record.

There have been some very interesting descriptions of the first coach. A recent Wikipedia entry describes Peebles as having "a twinkle in his eye, a moustache, winged collars and the bearing of a scholar, so that even on the field of play he looked as though he were en route to the court of St. James."

The first game that season was certainly interesting and played with some dispute. It took place in Northfield, Minnesota, against Carleton College. The Gophers' opponent insisted that a member of the faculty be allowed to play in the game, and that the game be played rugby style. Although Coach Peebles preferred the soccer style type play, he eventually agreed as long as he could serve as the game's referee. Carleton won 4-2. It doesn't seem likely that head coach Tim Brewster will take on the dual roles of coach and referee in any future Minnesota games. Michigan or Ohio State might have an objection.

Following the intriguing season under Tom Peebles, the University did not field a team for two years. In 1886, Frederick S. Jones was hired to teach physics and coach the football team. He lead the Gophers for three seasons, notching a 3-3 record. In three seasons under Jones, the team played only six games. Jones became known as the "Father of Minnesota Football."

Unlike Coach Peebles, Jones preferred the rugby style of football, in part for practical reasons. It seems that a man named Alfred F. Pillsbury arrived on campus and happened to own a new rugby ball, which was highly unusual back then. So Gopher football practiced the rugby style mostly because of the preferences of the man who owned the ball.

Although Jones only coached for three years, he remained very active in athletics at the University and helped to secure the land and funding for Northrop Field, the Gophers' first home field. Coach Jones was also responsible for signing Henry L. Williams to his football contract in 1900. Williams would remain head coach for 22 years.

Alfred Pillsbury became a well-known figure in Gopher football history. In 1886 there were no eligibility rules, which likely accounted for Pillsbury playing for the Gophers for eight seasons, of which he held the distinction of captain of the team for two.

One of the games that year was played against Shattuck in Faribault, Minnesota, and this turned out to be the game where the Gophers used the first play signals. They were not effective, however, as the Gophers lost by a score of 9-5. During the rematch in Minneapolis, spectators were charged admission for the first time.

The following season the Gophers played only two games, against the alumni and Minneapolis High School, winning both contests. The Gophers were short a man during the game against the high school team and were forced to recruit a student who had come to the game as a spectator. His name was William Walter "Pudge" Heffelinger. He played one season at Minnesota and then went on to Yale University, where he became one of the most recognized names in the early days of American football. Heffelinger would return to coach the Gophers in 1895.

The 1888 team was the last to be coached by Frederick Jones. His record against Shattuck that final year was 1-1, winning 14-0 and losing 16-8.

The 1889 season was the only season in which the Gophers used game coaches, dividing the duties between four different coaches. The team played four games that year and finished with three wins and one loss. The game coaches were Al McCord, D.W. McCord, Frank Heffelinger and Billy Morse.

During this season an attempt was made to schedule a home game against Michigan, but to no avail. The Wolverines wanted Minnesota to pay the $200 travel expenses but Minnesota management refused, so the game was never played. It was also the year that a football association was formed connecting the Gopher football team to the University student body. Without this association, the team had at times been forced to recruit from other schools in order to have enough players to compete.

Tom Eck was hired to coach during the 1890 season, an historic season because it featured the first meeting between Minnesota and Wisconsin, the most played rivalry in college football history. Minnesota won the opening contest 63-0. Except for 1906, the Gophers and the Badgers have met every year. The 1906 game was cancelled by President Theodore Roosevelt who had decided a "cooling off" period was necessary for college football because of injuries and deaths on the field.

The week before the Wisconsin game, Minnesota played another historic football game, the first game against an opponent outside of the state of Minnesota. They beat Grinnell 18-13. Tom Eck's only year of coaching the Gophers ended with a 5-1-1 record.

The following season Edward "Dad" Moulton became the head football coach and was another who coached only one season, finishing with a record of 3-1-1. During this season, the Gopher team took two out-of-state trips to Iowa, their first ever. It marked the beginning of the long rivalry against the neighboring Hawkeyes, and set up the eventual trophy battle for "Floyd of Rosedale."

The Gophers' 1892 season was played without a head coach. During this year an organization was formed that included representatives from Minnesota, Northwestern, Michigan and Wisconsin, called the Intercollegiate Athletic Association of the Northwest.

The Gophers won the first league championship that season by going undefeated and beating each of the Association members. The game that year against Michigan would begin a heated and historic rivalry, and eventually several years later bring about the most famous and coveted of all game trophies, The Little Brown Jug. Another first ever meeting took place against Northwestern. In addition to the Association wins, the Gophers also recorded victories over Grinnell and the Ex-Collegiates.

The Gophers also went undefeated during the 1893 season under head coach Wallie Winter. Coach Winter had been a tackle on the Yale football team and achieved All-American status. He was a tough football coach and was known to work the players very hard at practice. His squads had the reputation of saying the games were easy to play compared to the practices under the new head coach. Even though the team went undefeated again, it was the only season for Winter.

As the Gophers worked their way through the season without a loss, the final game of the year against Wisconsin would decide the Association championship. The Gophers proved to be so dominant that the contest was ended early, with Minnesota having a 40-0 lead. Unfortunately, after only two seasons in operation, financial problems forced the Association to disband. Over the two seasons it was a member, Minnesota won all six of its league games.

In 1894 Tom Cochrane, Jr., took over the Gophers as yet another one-year coach. His record as the headman was 3-1. Cochrane was also from Yale and in order to raise money for the team during tough financial times, he delivered lectures around the nation, giving a speech entitled "Football as Played in the East."

During Coach Cochrane's season, Minnesota made its very first trip to Madison, Wisconsin, to play the Badgers. The Badgers were a heavy underdog in the game, but were victorious by a 6-0 score in a hard fought win over the previously undefeated Gophers. It also marked the year the Gophers played Purdue for the first time.

Walter "Pudge" Heffelinger returned to Minnesota from a successful career at Yale and coached the Gophers for one year during the 1895 season, leading the team to a 7-3 record. It proved to be a historic year for Golden Gopher football, the last it would play as an independent. A group known as the Big Ten Conference had been formed, and Minnesota would join the following year.

The 1895 season also marked a major financial turnaround for the team, due to support from city businessmen and game attendance revenue. Gopher wins that season were over Minneapolis Central High School, the Boat Club, Macalester, and the Ex-Collegiates. Losses were to Grinnell, Purdue and Michigan.

In 1896, Alexander Jerrems became the Gopher's head coach and stayed for two seasons. He won 12 games and lost 6 and finished 1-5 during the Gophers' first two seasons of play in the newly-formed Big Ten Conference, which was also known as the Western Conference.

Jerrems had played halfback and fullback at Yale and led Minnesota to its first conference win against Purdue, but was unsuccessful in games against Michigan and Wisconsin.

The 1897 season marked the last for Coach Jerrems, as he lost the last four games of the season and was not asked to return the following year. The student newspaper reported that the lack of team success was attributed to poor team management. Several rule changes were implemented by the athletic program in 1897, including the decision that students would no longer choose managers.

Jack Minds, who had been an All-American fullback and kicker at the University of Pennsylvania, succeeded Alexander Jerrems at Minnesota. Minds lead the Gophers to a disappointing 4-5 record. Besides the win-loss record, the 1898 season also brought an injury to the team captain, a great deal of bad weather during the season, and a 5th place finish in the seven-team conference.

During a historic Thanksgiving Day battle against Illinois that year, the game was delayed several times due to the ball being lost in mammoth snowdrifts on the sides of the field. There had been an incredible snowstorm the previous day and it took valiant efforts by the student manager and a work crew to clear the field in order for the game to be played. Horse-drawn plows saved the cancellation of the contest, only to have the game eventually called due to temperatures falling to 10 degrees below zero before noon.

The next football season brought William C. Leary and John Harrison to the head coaching reins. The Gophers finished 6-3-2 that year but were 0-3 in Big Ten play. The team experimented with having two coaches, and although some considered it fairly successful, the practice was discontinued for the following year, which saw the hiring of the

Northrop Field was used for the first time during the 1899 season.

first full-time salaried coach.

Northrop Field, on the University of Minnesota campus, was used for the first time during the 1899 season. Governor John S. Pillsbury and Professor Fred Jones were credited for securing the home turf. All of the Gopher games that season were played on Northrop Field except for the final game, a loss to the University of Chicago at Marshall Field in Chicago.

In 1900, an historic era in Gopher football began with the hiring of Dr. Henry L. Williams as the new head football coach. He would remain for 22 seasons and compile a phenomenal record of 136 wins, 33 losses and 11 ties. He led the Gophers to a sole Big Ten championship in 1909 and 5 co-Big Ten championships in 1900, 1903, 1904, 1906 and 1915. Except for Wallie Winter, whose single-season record was 6-0, Coach Williams has the highest winning percentage of any Gopher football coach in history.

During the 1903 season, Williams' Gophers were 14-0-1, with the tie coming against a great Michigan team at Northrop Field. This was the game where Fielding Yost's Michigan team left behind their water jug, and the historic "Little Brown Jug" trophy was inaugurated. Coach Williams' prominence in Gopher lore is celebrated on the University of

Above: The 1903 Gophers squad finished 14-0-1.

Left: Dr. Henry L. Williams

Minnesota campus with the naming of Williams Arena for the legendary coach.

Coach Williams had coached for Army previously and began to build a solid record for Minnesota football, as his teams won on a regular basis. In Big Ten conference play under Williams, the Gophers were 50-25-5, while winning numerous championships.

During Williams' coaching years, 31 Gopher players were named to the All-Big Ten teams and 13 players were named All-Americans. During the 1902 season Minnesota defeated Grinnell by a score of 102-0, marking the first and only time the Gophers scored 100 plus points in a game. That same year the Gophers defeated Hamline 59-0, yet lost the final game of the season to rival Michigan 23-6 in Ann Arbor.

In 1913, Williams' Gopher squad featured fullback Clark Shaughnessy, who later would be credited for revolutionizing the way the game of football was played.

Williams was the first to propose the forward pass be a legal part of the game of football, and he also invented the 4-man defensive backfield, along with "Pudge" Heffelinger, an assistant coach on his staff. The "Minnesota shift," a term that found its way into football lore, was also introduced by Coach Williams and his Gopher teams.

The roster of the 1915 team, co-Big Ten champions, included such legendary players as Bert Baston and Bernie Bierman. Baston, Bierman and guard Meron Dunningham were selected to the All-American team that year.

Henry Williams' final season at Minnesota was 1921.

William Spaulding was named head coach following Williams, leading the team during the 1922-1924 seasons. He compiled an 11-7-4 record with a 5-6-3 Big Ten conference record. The 1923 season produced a 5-1-1 record and would be the final season of play for the Gophers at Northrop Field. The following year, Memorial Stadium became the new home for Minnesota football.

On November 15, 1924, the Gophers hosted Illinois in their dedication game for the new stadium; however they actually opened the season in the new stadium against North Dakota on October 7, 1924, with a 22-0 victory.

Clarence Spears served as head coach for a five-year period followed Spaulding, from 1925-1929. He had a great record, accumulating 28 wins, only 9 losses and 3 ties. Spears had six players named All-Americans and 15 named to the All-Big Ten team.

Spears had been an All-American guard at Dartmouth and followed his Minnesota tenure with head coaching positions at Oregon, Wisconsin, Toledo and Maryland. His final year at Minnesota boasted the legendary Bronko Nagurski as the team's fullback and tackle, and he achieved All-American status at both positions. The story of how Spears recruited Bronko remains one of the great Gopher legends. Gopher historians claim Nagurski raised a plow with his bare hands to point out directions to a lost Spears near the Nagurski home.

In 1930, the new head football coach at Minnesota was future Michigan legend Herbert "Fritz" Crisler. Crisler remained at Minnesota for only two seasons, posting a 10-7-1 record.

Crisler coached Biggie Munn, the great Gopher All-American guard who later went on to coach at Michigan State University and developed a heated intra-state rivalry with his former coach. Munn remained at Michigan State as athletic director for almost two decades following his retirement from coaching, serving as AD until 1971. Biggie Munn was inducted into the "M" Club Hall of Fame in 1993.

In 1932, a legendary time at the University of Minnesota began with the hiring of head football coach Bernie Bierman. Coach Bierman would lead the Gophers to five national championships-in 1934, 1935, and 1936 and again in 1940 and 1941. He would coach the Gophers for a total of 16 years from 1932-1941 and again from 1945-1950.

Biernie Bierman was born in Springfield, Minnesota, on March 11, 1894 and died in 1977. Before coming to Minnesota as the head coach, he coached at Montana, Mississippi State, and the University of Tulane. While at Minnesota, Bierman won 93 games, lost 35 and tied 6.

In addition to the five national championships, Bierman posted six Big Ten titles and five undefeated seasons. During his seasons at Minnesota, he coached 21 players to All-American status, and 36 players made the All-Big Ten team.

In 1934, the Gophers began an unforgettable run, amassing a three-year record of 23 wins and one loss, and three consecutive national

championship seasons. In 1940 and again in 1941, the Gophers reclaimed the national championship.

Bierman left the Gophers after the 1941 season for military obligations and returned as head coach in 1945, where he remained in charge for six more seasons.

During Bierman's three-year hiatus from coaching, George Hauser led the Gophers. Hauser's teams had a record of 15-11-1, and they went 8-8-1 in conference games.

During the 1942 season, the Gophers hosted the U.S. Navy Pre-Flight School at the University of Iowa. The military squad was coached by a familiar name to Minnesota fans, Bernie Bierman. It must have been quite the reunion.

George Hauser coached All-American Dick Wildung, and in 1943 he coached All-Americans Bill Daley and Herb Hein. In the late 1940s Bierman would coach some of the greatest players to ever wear the maroon and gold: Billy Bye, Bud Grant, Leo Nomellini and Clayton Tonnemaker.

The Bernie Bierman era came to an end at the conclusion of the 1950 season, and Wesley Eugene "Wes" Fesler became the new head coach of the Golden Gophers. Fesler was a great athlete at Ohio State and had been a three-time All-American. He coached at Pittsburgh, Wesleyan and Ohio State before coming to Minnesota.

Fesler coached 1950 Heisman Trophy winner Vic Janowicz at Ohio State and Paul Giel at Minnesota in 1952 and 1953. But Fesler did not win enough games as head coach and was replaced after only three years.

In 1954, the University of Minnesota hired Murray Warmath as its head football coach. There was little known about Coach Warmath when he came to Minnesota for the 1954 season. Coming from the Deep South, Warmath had played at Tennessee for legendary coach Robert Neyland and had coached at Mississippi State for two seasons. He served as the head coach of the Gophers for eighteen seasons.

In a book on Murray Warmath entitled *The Autumn Warrior*, published by Burgess International Group in 1992, author Mike Wilkenson chronicles the career of Warmath based on many hours of discussion

---

Bernie Bierman had a career record at Minnesota of 93-35-6 with five national championships.

with the coach.

Wilkenson says, "First, there is probably no one alive today, with the exception of Sid Gillman, who has been so directly involved in the game of football for so many years. Beginning as a high school player in the late 1920s in Humboldt, Tennessee, until today, [Warmath] has followed a unique path for six decades in the game he so dearly loves.

Second, there is no one who saved his job in such dramatic fashion as he did in 1960 when he won the national championship and took the University of Minnesota Golden Gophers to the first of two consecutive Rose Bowls. From late 1957 through the end of the 1959 season, the Monday morning quarterbacks were asking for his hide. What they didn't know was that he knew more about football than all of them combined and he knew better days were just ahead. He was certainly right.

Third, he was a major force, if not the major force in the advent of the black athlete in collegiate football in the late 1950s and early 1960s. As a white southerner in a time when segregation ruled the south, it was both noticeable and unusual for something of that magnitude to happen. However, those who know Murray Warmath know that he judges people on things far more important than their race, religion or creed.

Fourth, he coached an incredible number of young men who went on to be very successful in later life. In a time when college sports is often criticized for churning out athletes who are ill-equipped to deal with demands away from the playing fields, courts or rinks, Warmath has had the satisfaction of seeing so many of his players become leaders in medicine, law, business, education and coaching. While their successes are mainly of their own doing, to a man they will tell you that Warmath was a major figure in their lives and a role model who set a wonderful example of how character, integrity and dedication pay off in all aspects of life.

Finally, Warmath is a man of the highest principles. He is a devoted family man, much in love with, and deeply appreciative of, his wonderful wife of over 50 years, Mary Louise, his children and his grandchildren. He is a classic no-nonsense guy. He expects nothing more from others than he asks of himself. He is extraordinarily fair and honest. A tireless and detail-oriented worker, it is clear that he would have been successful in any endeavor. Fortunately for those who love football, he chose coaching. It is my fondest hope that this book will not only give its readers a history of this man, but also make them full aware of what a wonderful person he is and appreciative of all he has given of himself."

During the time that Warmath coached at Minnesota, he won 87 games, lost 78 and tied 7. His 1960 team won the national championship and he led the Gophers to the Rose Bowl in 1961 and 1962.

In Murray Warmath's first season as head coach, the Gophers featured the running of All-American Bob McNamara, and Warmath's Gophers finished the season ranked 20th in the nation by the UPI poll.

As noted in *The Autumn Warrior*, Warmath was credited as the first coach to bring black athletes north to play football. It was his leadership in this regard that essentially broke the collegiate color barrier for black athletes to be recruited and travel to northern colleges to play football.

The 1955 season was a difficult year for the maroon and gold. The Gophers won only three games and lost 6, notching a 2-5 record in the Big Ten.

On October 22, 1955, the Gophers played host to number-one ranked Michigan and held a 13-7 half time lead. The old Peach Section of the *Minneapolis Tribune* sent out an early edition with the headlines announcing the Gopher half time lead, but it was for naught. The great Michigan team came on to score a touchdown in the second half and held on for a victory.

The 1956 team had high expectations, especially with quarterback Bobby Cox and All-American tackle Bob Hobart. Attendance was up, with the team averaging 62,109, and Minnesota was ranked 9th in the country by the UPI poll. The team finished the season with an overall record of 6-1-2, and 4-1-2 in the Big Ten.

The next three seasons were very tough on the Gophers and their fans. A total of just seven wins meant many were calling for the firing of Coach Warmath. He was not treated well by the Gopher faithful, but at the time no one knew that a trip to the Rose Bowl and the national championship were on the horizon.

Dick Cullum, former writer for the *Minneapolis Tribune*, captured the essence of what the coach went through during those difficult years.

In *The Autumn Warrior*, Cullum is quoted as saying, "While the subject is still alive, I'd like to say something about my friend, Murray Warmath. The manner in which he has conducted himself in these trying times has been so much that of a gentleman that it must shame those that attacked him with malice and with disregard of the underlying facts.

I do not hesitate to say I do not know a man, in any field of endeavor, who had greater character. Who can have greater character than a man that has it all? Through these many years I have never known him to do a small, malicious, or harmful thing.

Someone said he has shown a lot of courage.

Yes, I suppose that is so, but I don't think he has ever had to draw on courage. Instead, his flawless character caused him to do the right thing without ever having to back it up with courage. There has never been, for him, more than one course of action, more than one decision to be made.

His character dictated the act or the decision. He never considered a second choice and his choice was right because there was a lucid mind behind his character.

In particular, I must say that, measuring these qualities, he so distinctly outclasses those who have attacked him with malice that he makes these people hard to tolerate.

Let them show any part of the same character and competence, or pause for a while for self examination."

Under Coach Warmath, the Gophers won the national championship in 1960, went to two consecutive Rose Bowls in 1961 and 1962, and tied for the Big Ten championship in 1967. The team had some great players on its roster. Bob Stein was named All-American twice and Aaron Brown also earned the honor. Others, such as tackle John Williams and defensive back Tom Sakal, proved to be powerful players. Charlie Sanders, a tremendous tight end for Minnesota, went on to a prolific professional career and was recently voted into the Professional Football Hall of Fame.

Murray Warmath's final season as head coach of the Minnesota Gophers was in 1971, and he won just four games that year. His team featured All-American Doug Kingriter and linebacker Bill Light. Warmath stayed on at the University in the athletic department and later became a line coach for the Vikings under Bud Grant.

During Coach Warmath's years at the Gopher helm, he coached nine All-American players: Bob McNamara (1954); Bob Hobart (1956); Tom Brown (1960); Sandy Stephens (1961); Bobby Bell (1961 and 1962); Carl

Eller (1963); Aaron Brown (1965); Bob Stein (1967 and 1968); and Doug Kingriter (1971). He coached 23 All Big Ten players, two Outland Trophy winners in Tom Brown and Bobby Bell, and College Football Hall of Famers in Bell, Brown and Eller.

At the age of 96, Coach Warmath still attends many local football functions and goes to all the Gopher football games. He is held in great regard by his former players and interacts with them often. A family friend notes that Warmath is proud of the relationships he has with his players. Former players often respond to questions from the coach with "Yes sir" and "no sir." The coach lights up at football gatherings; he loves Gopher football and all those who played for him. Coach Tim Brewster, no matter what the gathering, points out the presence of Coach Warmath and relishes recounting the coach's accomplishments.

"He still gives me tips on how to build our defense," says Brewster, who is proud to have Warmath near. It is a great relationship.

Murray Warmath still bleeds the maroon and gold colors. He is a legend, a national champion coach, and a beloved leader. As Coach Brewster proudly says, "Coach Warmath executed the greatest story in the history of college football. No team had ever gone from last place in their conference (1959) to winning the national championship the following season (1960). Coach Murray Warmath and his Gophers did."

In 1972, the new coach at Minnesota was Cal Stoll. Stoll came from Wake Forest where he had been the head football coach from 1969-1971. Stoll's record with the Gophers was 39 wins and 39 losses during his seven years as the head coach.

The Gophers had some very good teams during the Stoll era and featured such notable players as Rick Upchurch, Steve Neils, Keith Fahnhorst, Matt Herkenhoff, Tony Dungy, George Adzick, Steve Midboe, Paul Rogind, Marion Barber, Jr., and Kent Kitzmann, who once carried the football 56 times in one game, a Gopher record.

One of the great victories in the history of Minnesota football came in 1977, as the Gophers defeated number-one ranked and powerful Michigan at the Brick House by a score of 16-0.

Former Coach Murray Warmath was the WCCO radio color commentator during the game and gave an awe-inspiring analysis after the game, relative to how a powerhouse like Michigan could lose such an important Big Ten conference match-up against the underdog Gophers. It was bril-

liant.

"They had been told all week by their coaches to look out for Minnesota," said Warmath. "But when you win like they had been winning, the players do not believe it is possible to lose to a team like Minnesota. And that's how you lose those games."

Cal Stoll was fired after the 1978 season and Minnesota hired former Gopher quarterback and assistant coach Joe Salem to take over the head coaching duties. Salem, extremely well liked and with a successful coaching resume, had a tough time at the helm and finished with an overall record of 19-35-1 and conference record of 12-32-1 during his five seasons as head coach.

Salem coached some outstanding players during his short tenure, including Elmer Bailey, Mark Carlson, Gary White, Jeff Schuh and Marion Barber, Jr. In the early 1980s, Coach Salem had notables Jim Fahnhorst and Ken Dallafior in the lineup along with prolific passer Mike Hohensee. The 1983 season was the last for Joe Salem, as the Gophers won their first game, but suffered defeat in the remaining ten.

Minnesota hired Lou Holtz to coach the Gophers in 1984, and hope returned with the hype and promises of Holtz. He resurrected the belief that Minnesota could win again, with an outstanding performance and close loss to mighty and highly-ranked Oklahoma.

Ricky Foggie was a great player for the Gophers during the Holtz reign, and after two seasons hope had been returned to the loyalists. Then suddenly and with seemingly little warning, Lou Holtz left for the head-coaching job at Notre Dame. Fans learned that Holtz's contract included a clause that allowed him to leave Minnesota if he was offered the head coaching position at Notre Dame. Holtz had proven at Minnesota that he was a great football coach, and the loss of his leadership after two seasons was difficult to take.

During his time at Minnesota, Holtz's 10-12 win/loss record was enough to make the believers believe again. He did a fabulous job in taking the Gopher squad to new heights with a very promising future ahead. It certainly would have been interesting to see what would have occurred if Holtz had remained for a decade or two.

Cal Stoll and Tony Dungy.

Lou Holtz brought back hope for the Minnesota faithful during the 1984-85 seasons.

In 1986, the University hired one of Lou Holtz's successful assistants, John Gutekunst, to take over as the head coach of the Gophers. Gutekunst was the players' favorite to replace Holtz, but he had a difficult time matching Holtz in keeping the Gophers' championship dreams alive.

Gutekunst finished his five-year stint with the Gophers with an overall record of 29-36-2, and although a very popular coach, he was not retained after the Gophers failed to show improvement.

After Holtz left in 1985, Gutekunst did lead the Gophers to a 20-13 win in the Independence Bowl. In 1986, his first year as head coach, he took them to the Liberty Bowl but lost 28-21.

The Gutekunst teams had many outstanding players, including running back and all-time leading rusher Darrell Thompson, kicker Chip Lohmiller, guard Troy Wilkow and center Chris Thome. In 1991, Coach Gutekunst's final season with the Gophers, his squad finished with a record of 2-9.

Jim Wacker was hired to coach the Gophers, beginning with the 1992 season.

Wacker had been a successful head coach at Texas Christian University and was known throughout football circles as a man with tremendous enthusiasm and integrity. Wacker's coaching resume included successful tenures at Texas Lutheran, North Dakota State and TCU, winning four national championships during his career and earning National Coach of the Year honors while at TCU. Minnesota football earned the nickname "Air Wacker" for a time, as Coach Wacker really liked to throw the football.

However, Jim Wacker was not as successful with the Gophers as he had been in his previous coaching assignments. His record was only 16 wins with 39 losses; he had a conference record of 8-32. Wacker's teams included 1994 All-Big Ten First Team members Ed Hawthorne and Chris Darkins.

Wacker's final year with the Gophers was 1996. Though well-liked, Wacker could not lead the Gophers into the Big Ten elite nor return them to national prominence.

Jim Wacker finished his coaching career with an overall coaching mark of 160-130-3. He became athletic director at Southwest Texas in 1998. Wacker died in 2003 after a long battle with cancer, and Southwest Texas has named the field inside Bobcat Stadium in Jim Wacker's honor.

Glen Mason became the next head coach of the Gophers in 1997 and remained with the football team as the head coach for 10 seasons. In 1999, he won Big Ten Coach of the Year honors. Mason played college football at Ohio State University. He had extensive experience as an assistant coach and had been the head coach at Kent State and at Kansas.

In January of 2002, Mason was named President of the American Football Coaches Association, following in the footsteps of Bernie Bierman and Murray Warmath.

During the 10 years that Mason coached the Gophers, he won 64 games and lost 57, going 32-48 in Big Ten play. Mason coached 11 players to All-American status and had 24 players achieve All-Big Ten status. Mason also coached the Gophers in seven bowl games, winning three and losing four. After the bowl game at the conclusion of the 2006 season, Glen Mason was let go as head coach of the Gophers and was soon replaced by Tim Brewster. Glen Mason is doing commentary on the Big Ten Network and working in the financial industry in the Twin

Cities.

Since Tom Peebles took the reins as head football coach of the Minnesota Golden Gophers in 1883, a total of 30 coaches have served as the head coach of Gopher football, and they have accumulated 628 total wins and 454 losses with 44 tie scores. It is a remarkable record. In the process, there have been six national championships; only three major universities hold claim to more.

Gopher football fans have been fortunate to have had their football team led by honorable men who have given their best on and off the field to represent the University of Minnesota. It has been a great run in over a century of play, but there are titles and championships out there waiting for the Gophers to claim. And at this time their fortune rests in the hands of Gopher head football coach Tim Brewster.

Overhead shot of Memorial Stadium.

9

BACK TO CAMPUS

There were those that cried when the old Memorial Stadium was torn down. And there were even some tears shed during the near decade that it was left vacant after the Gophers moved off campus and into the Metrodome in downtown Minneapolis.

Memorial Stadium had seemingly been there forever, though Gopher historians know it came into existence in 1924, when the Gophers moved from their first home at Greater Northrop Field.

Memorial Stadium served as the backdrop for some of the greatest teams and players in Minnesota football history. It housed the men who wore the maroon and gold and the fans who came to watch them play on those Saturday afternoons in the fall.

Memorial Stadium was where Bernie Bierman roamed the sidelines with his championship teams of the 1930s and 1940s. It housed the undefeated seasons and the greatest turnaround in college football histo-

ry, when the Warmath squad of 1960 rose from the depths of the Big Ten to win the national championship and head to the Rose Bowl. It housed the names of Nagurski, Baston, Grant, and Smith, and was the setting of some of the great victories over bitter rival Michigan.

And the old stadium was incredible. Walking down the steps of Cooke Hall and gazing into the back of the temporary bleachers provided a view into the great facility. The white chalk lines, the running track and the goal posts, all waiting peacefully for the beloved Gophers. It was magnificent.

The towering stands held over 60,000, and when filled made for a splendid sight. On a beautiful autumn Saturday, the atmosphere was extraordinary, and the Gopher faithful appreciated their football tradition.

It didn't matter from which direction you approached the grand old stadium; there was something truly reverent about it. The approach was filled with the anticipation of something special. The stadium was central to football on campus, housed among the fraternity houses on University Avenue.

Around the corner from the Brick House and sitting behind Cooke Hall was the Gopher practice field, the old Northrop Field. Massive in field space and adjacent to the parking ramp, informally referred to as Mollenkopf Towers, Northrop was where the Gophers spent so many afternoons during the fall.

If you ever had the opportunity to walk out of the Gopher locker room, you would have had to make a quick turn to the left in order to move toward the field at Memorial. If you walked directly out of the locker room and went straight ahead, you would hit a solid wall rising to the parking lot near Cooke Hall. It was a place that fans often gathered to watch the Golden Gophers come out of the locker room and go on to the field.

One Saturday in the mid-60s an unusual thing occurred in a pivotal game against the University of Missouri.

Dan Devine, head coach of the Tigers, had brought his favored squad in to battle the Gophers, and both teams were out on the field when a light drizzle started. At the conclusion of the warm-up period, the Gophers entered their locker room and began final preparations for kick off.

The weather changed dramatically in the few minutes the team was off the field; the light drizzle began to freeze after hitting solid surfaces. The boardwalk outside the Gopher's locker room that led to the field became a sheet of ice.

At that time, football cleats were vinyl with metal tips, not a great combination to ensure footing on a slippery wooden surface. The team gathered together to hear Murray Warmath's pre-game talk. Warmath had a gift for delivering the right message at the right time. And he didn't disappoint this time. The Gophers stormed out of the locker room toward the field to take on the Missouri squad.

It is a good thing that those in the stands on that rainy Saturday and those on the opposing side of the field did not see what next occurred. Unfortunately, all of the fans gathered at the top of the parking lot looking down on the Gophers coming out of the locker room did see what happened.

The first Gopher roared out of the locker room, ready to hit anything that moved, but as he tried to make the left turn to the field his feet flew out from underneath him. One by one the maroon and gold slipped and slid, piling over, around, and under each other as the fans watched in dismay.

Once back on their feet, the wet and embarrassed team headed to the field to do battle. It was a bad start and it didn't get better as the Warmath squad fell victim to Devine and his Missouri team by the score of 17-6.

It was a hard fought football game and the Gophers played decently, although the team's entrance on to the field may have foreshadowed the outcome. It was a loss, but it was also Gopher football, in the rain and the cold, outside and on campus where it was meant to be played.

***

The old locker room under the stadium had its own history, as many of the great Gopher players dressed there. For many years there was an old blackboard on the wall where the lineups were posted before the games. Bell, Eller, Brown, Hankinson, Peterson, Wintermute, Rosen, Larson, Sakal, Stein and the others were all there.

And at the back of the locker room, slightly up from the main floor, was where a group of players gathered before games and practices. They wouldn't play much, not see a lot of action, yet were still Gophers. They ran the opposing teams' offenses and defenses during practices, but didn't participate much in the Saturday games. They were called the "Bombers," and each Bomber played a role on the Gopher squads.

For a time, the end of the season featured a special day at the old stadium for the players and their dads. It was "Dad's Day" and each of the players' fathers was given special treatment. A luncheon and a place on the field next to the team was all a part of it. And each of the dads sat on the bench wearing his son's number. It was a great day at the Brick House.

And on each of those Saturdays when football was played at Memorial Stadium, the campus came alive. The walk to the stadium down University Avenue, the smell of the hot dogs and hot coffee and the first look at the field from the entrance ramps was unforgettable.

And then it all changed as the Gophers abandoned their home after almost six decades and headed for the Metrodome in downtown

Minneapolis.

The atmosphere changed. There was no grass and no fraternity houses. There was no walk down University Avenue. And the home of the
Gophers was really no longer a place to be called home, as others also
shared the facility. It was bright, rather plastic in nature and appearance,
and no one got dirty. There would no longer be the grass stains on the
jerseys, no mud and dirt testament to playing at Memorial Stadium.

The marching band did its best to create the game day atmosphere,
but it was just not the same. For most of the games, many seats
remained empty. The Gophers' losing record didn't help with attendance,
but even the occasional big game didn't fill the seats.

You weren't able to stroll past the Gopher practice field waiting for
game time at the Metrodome because there was no practice field nearby.
There was no Cooke Hall and no field house. The fact was the Gophers
were playing a home game off of the University of Minnesota campus,
and everything about the collegiate experience for a home football game
had disappeared.

But now it is going to all change.

The Minnesota Golden Gophers football team is coming home to
TCF Bank Stadium to play football on campus once again. The game
will return to the outdoors and the fans will be on University Avenue
again, on the way to the game.

The students will walk across campus, past Northrup Auditorium,
past Coffman Union, past the giant field house, out of the fraternity
houses and to the game. They will gather outside the massive new structure and enjoy the atmosphere, the anticipation, the gala, and all that
goes with Gopher football on Saturday afternoons. After 27 seasons, the
Gophers are coming home.

It likely won't take very long for the Gophers to start winning again.

"It's the missing piece," says Gopher head football coach Tim
Brewster. "The stadium is the missing piece."

Aerial photo of the Metrodome in 2006.

10

THE STADIUM

As you traveled down University Avenue from the west toward the University of Minnesota campus, it used to loom above from the left. They called it the Brick House. It was a massive oval horseshoe-shaped structure that was the home of the Golden Gophers football team from 1924-1981. It's gone.

Now as you travel down University Avenue from the west toward the University of Minnesota campus, it rises above you from the right. They call it TCF Bank Stadium. It is a massive oval horseshoe-shaped structure and is the new home of the Golden Gophers football team beginning in the fall of 2009. And what is its significance? It has brought the University of Minnesota football team home once again, the greatest comeback in Gopher history!

When the Minnesota Gophers first started playing collegiate football, they didn't have a home field. At the time the Gophers traveled to several places to play their games.

Some games were played on campus fields and others around the Minneapolis area. The team also played on a field next to the University of Minnesota Armory and at the downtown Athletic Park, next to the West Hotel. However, from 1882-1898 there was no permanent home for the maroon and gold.

But in 1899 things would change, as the first home field for the Gophers came into being. It was called Northrop Field, named in honor of University of Minnesota President Cyrus Northrop. The field remained the home for Minnesota football through the 1923 season, the last before the Gophers moved to the newly-built Memorial Stadium nearby. It was nothing like the modern fields of today's collegiate football arenas, but it accommodated the Gophers and established a home field advantage. It represented the pride and tradition of Minnesota football.

Northrop Field, named after Minnesota President Cyrus Northrop, had a seating capacity of 20,000.

Originally, Northrop's seating capacity was about 3,000, but in 1902 the field was moved in order to add additional seating, bringing the game day attendance to 20,000. Due to this tremendous capacity increase, after 1902 the field was referred to as Greater Northrop Field.

In 1903, the first season with the increased seating, the Gophers battled Michigan in the game that has come to be known as the Little Brown Jug game. When the Gophers moved into Memorial Stadium in 1924, Northrop Field became a practice field for the team and a site for other University events.

At one point a parking ramp was built adjacent to the field. It wasn't long before the ramp was given a name by those closely connected to the football program; it was referred to as Mollenkopf Towers, named after former Purdue football coach Jack Mollenkopf.

Legend has it that Coach Murray Warmath was not in favor of the ramp because it provided a site from which an interested party could oversee Gopher football practices.

As the tale goes, one day former ball boy and later assistant coach Tim McGovern actually caught one of the Purdue assistant football coaches filming a Gopher practice from the parking ramp. That incident gave the ramp its infamous name.

Memorial Stadium opened on October 14, 1924. The new home field for the Gophers was dedicated to 3,527 students, graduates and workers who had served in World War I. The stadium sat on approximately 11 acres on the University of Minnesota campus. And it was a beautiful football setting. The great horseshoe created a perfect atmosphere for Big Ten football.

During the time that it served as home to the Golden Gophers, the famous Brick House hosted six national championship teams, 17 Big Ten conference championships, numerous All-Americans and an abundance of great coaches, including the legendary likes of Henry Williams, Bernie Bierman and Murray Warmath, who coached the Gophers for a combined 56 years.

Memorial Stadium would prove to be one of the great college football

stadiums in America during its prime, and it was the site for some of the greatest college football games ever played. In 1940, the great Michigan team led by Tom Harmon came to Memorial Stadium only to be stopped on a muddy, rain-soaked field by an immortal Gopher squad, as the maroon and gold won the national championship 7-6. It was the day of the legendary 80-yard run by future Heisman Trophy winner Bruce Smith, fulfilling his father's wish for vengeance against the Michigan team that had defeated the Gophers for the national championship some 30 years earlier.

It was the place that Tom Brown manhandled the Iowa center in the 1960 Iowa game, and the legendary Sandy Stephens led the Gophers to victory and the national championship that same year.

The dynasty built by the legendary Bernie Bierman teams and the great running of Paul Giel and Bob McNamara brought the crowds to their feet many times in the 1950s, as did the immortal Bobby Bell and Carl Eller as they led the great Gopher teams of the early 60s.

In the 1970s, the stadium had an official seating capacity of 56,652. Temporary bleachers could increase seating to approximately 66,000. Memorial Stadium had a track running around the field and also served as the track and field venue for other Gopher teams, and on one occasion in 1969, due to a baseball conflict with the Twins, the Minnesota Vikings played the Green Bay Packers in a regular season game at the stadium. They also played a pre-season game there in 1971.

But the atmosphere, the tradition of the old stadium, the great teams and players of the past didn't seem to be enough for some, and the thought of moving the team to a new home began to be entertained.

Pressured by downtown Minneapolis business interests and some powerful athletic boosters, the University made the decision to move out of the stadium in the spring of 1982 and into the Metrodome, which was approximately two miles away from campus.

Athletic director Paul Giel supported the move, noting that sharing the home with the Minnesota Vikings would be advantageous to recruiting and eliminate problems with typical late-autumn weather conditions.

In order to assure that the Minnesota Gophers would not return to Memorial Stadium, the University proposed an indoor swimming pool

Memorial Stadium opened on October 14, 1924.

that would extend into the stadium at the open end; however legal challenges halted construction, so the school planned an alternative for the stadium site.

In 1990 a new Aquatic Center opened and two years later, Memorial Stadium was torn down. All that was left of the great brick structure was the original brick entrance arch. When the McNamara Alumni Center was built on the same site, the massive arch remained in the interior atrium over the entrance to the small museum, as a remembrance of the great stadium and the games played there.

In 1982, the Golden Gophers left the Brick House and the campus and moved into the Metrodome for their home games. It proved to be a huge disappointment to the team, the fans and the University. The off-campus site lacked the college atmosphere, and the Gophers were obliged to concede scheduling priority to both the Vikings and the Twins. The University also suffered the loss of revenue from concessions and park-

The Metrodome served as home for the Gopher football team for 27 seasons.

ing. Still, the Metrodome would be the home of Gopher football from 1982-2008, a total of 27 seasons.

Of course, the Metrodome did house a few memorable moments in Gopher football history. In 1984 and 1985, Lou Holtz brought hope back to the faithful with his passion for college football and his record for turning mediocre football teams into powerhouses. He had a fantastic ability to recruit outstanding players and was a reputable football coach.

"We are going to recruit the heart and soul of this football team from the state of Minnesota," proclaimed Holtz, "but we are going after the arms and legs from other places."

Holtz made the breakfast and luncheon circuits in the two years that he was here, rallying fan interest to a level that had not been seen in the area in many years. He promised a turn around in Gopher fortunes, and he backed up his words. He got everyone excited about Gopher football.

The year before Holtz arrived, 62, 687 fans trekked to the Dome to watch the Gophers fall to mighty Nebraska 84-13. The next week 41,839 showed up to see a loss to Purdue. And only 35,514 were in attendance for a 50-23 obliteration by Illinois. But Holtz brought it back. Attendance started to rise as fans sensed change in the air.

Lou Holtz had people believing again. On September 28, 1985, 62,446 filled the Dome as the Gophers took on number one-ranked Oklahoma. The Gophers battled the great Sooner team to the end, falling 13-7 but throwing the ball in the Sooner end zone on the final play, trying to pull out a last-second miracle. Holtz and his maroon and gold almost had them beat and most fans were ready to grant the team a moral victory. Holtz inspired both players and fans to a level the Gophers had not felt in a long time.

Gopher fans long desired to return to the big time in college football, and Lou Holtz was about to lead the parade. Gopher football was reborn. But just as fast as Holtz restored faith and hope, he was gone, off to South Bend to lead the Fighting Irish to the national championship, a championship many had hoped would belong to the maroon and gold.

But even with the disappointment of Lou Holtz's departure, there were some memorable games in the Metrodome. Many of those games involved the Gophers and the Purdue Boilermakers in high scoring contests.

On October 9, 1993, Purdue came to town and racked up 56 points.

They lost. Yes, the Golden Gophers won that incredible shoot-out by scoring 59 points and establishing eight new school records. Gopher quarterback Scott Eckers threw for 402 yards and six touchdown passes, five of those to receiver Omar Douglas. With both teams scoring almost at will throughout the game, it wasn't until the final eight seconds and a Mike Chalberg game-winning field goal that the Gophers sealed the win. A total of 1,184 yards were recorded on that crazy football afternoon in a game that will likely never be forgotten.

The Boilermakers and Gophers battled in another historic game in the Metrodome on October 7, 1995, when the Gophers went for a two-point conversion in the closing two minutes to cap a 38-37 win over Purdue. Gopher quarterback Cory Sauter led the team 66 yards in the final minutes and used a quarterback sneak with 1:38 on the clock to get Minnesota within one. Running back Chris Darkins rushed for an incredible 294 yards, a school record, with 232 of those yards coming in the second half.

It was 11th-ranked Purdue again on September 24, 2005, that the Gophers were able to overcome 42-35 in a double overtime victory. Bryan Cupito, the Gophers' record-setting quarterback, connected with receiver Logan Payne to tie the game on a fourth-down play in the first overtime. In the second overtime, Gary Russell scored on a touchdown run for the win. Lawrence Maroney, running back for Minnesota, totaled 333 all-purpose yards.

Wisconsin, Minnesota's neighbor to the east, also provided some great Dome contests. In 1993, the Gophers defeated the 15th-ranked Badgers 28-21 by intercepting five passes. Ten years later, in 2003, Gopher kicker Rhys Lloyd converted on a 35-yard field goal as time ran out for a Gopher win. Lawrence Maroney carried the ball 43 times for 258 yards before 65,089 in a losing effort against Wisconsin in 2005.

Darrell Thompson, Minnesota's all-time leading rusher, set the school record against Michigan on November 22, 1987, with a 98-yard touchdown run, running for 157 of his 201 yards in the first half of play. Cory Sauter threw for 397 yards against Ball State and Ryan Thelwell caught eight passes for 228 yards and a school record in a 1996 victory, and two-time All-American Tyrone Carter set a school record with two fumble recoveries for touchdowns in a Gopher win over favored Syracuse on September 21, 1996. On November 22, 1986, Gopher kicker Chip

Lohmiller broke the school record and established the second longest field goal in Big Ten history with an unbelievable 62-yard kick through the uprights against Iowa.

The Dome also housed the Gophers when Tutu Atwell shocked the fans with two kick off returns for touchdowns against Iowa State. He accounted for a Gopher record performance of 349 all-purpose yards for the game. In 2001, fans were delighted to see Gopher receiver Ron Johnson set the all-time Gopher record for pass receiving when he caught four passes, which accounted for his 46th consecutive game in which he had caught a pass.

Overall, the Dome atmosphere was the home environment for 88 wins, 79 losses and two ties. In Big Ten play the record for the Gophers at the Metrodome was 41-65-2. The best the Gophers did in their 27 years off campus was a third place finish in 1986; however, they finished in last place a total of nine times. While making the Metrodome their home, the Gophers did make nine Bowl appearances, winning four and losing five.

The dome concept originated many decades earlier, after the Vikings came into existence and the Twins moved to the Twin Cities.

Robert Cerny, a Minneapolis architect, first considered the idea of a domed stadium in downtown Minneapolis in the late 60s, which became a real political issue. Proposals for doming Memorial Stadium or Metropolitan Stadium or building a new facility at the State Fair Grounds or other sites were all discussed before a final decision was made. The $55 million Metrodome was inflated on October 2, 1981, and the stadium was completed in April of 1982. The Gophers officially moved in for the 1982 season.

With poor revenues and a significant lack of a collegiate atmosphere, the University of Minnesota began as early as 2002 to identify the need for a new on-campus football stadium. Over the course of the next few years various plans and ideas fell through.

However in December of 2005, the University and TCF Bank came forward with a deal which would give TCF naming rights to the stadium in return for $35 million towards the stadium project.

Through most of 2005, the University spent considerable time drafting various proposals that would draw support from state political leaders. A final agreement was reached with the understanding that the

University would raise 52% of the monies needed with the balance coming from the state. Funding was also planned to come from the sale of University land, student fees, corporate and private donations and game day parking.

The 2005 legislative session had given the proposal serious consideration, but the session ended without a bill to fund the stadium. However, because there had been considerable positive attention to the stadium funding, the University and TCF extended their original agreement through the 2006 session, and the momentum that had been previously in place resulted in the funding being approved.

The Governor signed the action for funding approval into law after the legislature passed final action on May 20, 2006, providing funding for a new University of Minnesota football stadium to be built on campus.

The original stadium site for Memorial Stadium could not be used due to the building of the Aquatic Center and the McNamara Alumni Center, so it was designed for a site approximately three blocks from where the old stadium once stood.

University President Robert Bruininks is a life long fan of Golden Gopher football. He attended games at the old Memorial Stadium and made a strong commitment to bring Gopher football back to campus when he became president in 2002.

"It was a very personal cause of mine to make every effort to return football back to campus," says President Bruininks. "It provides a magnificent opportunity to connect the people of the state to the University, our greatest state institution. We know from experience and research that half of the people who have connections and involvement do so through athletics. The stadium enhances every aspect of this relationship."

President Bruininks appointed a stadium planning committee in 2002 that met every week for the past seven years to bring the stadium plan to fruition.

"We have dreamed about what the stadium would be and it has now become a reality," says Bruininks. "I am most proud of the fact that it symbolizes the great state of Minnesota and will become a wonderful gathering place for people to meet. It represents the state so well with all 87 counties recognized within the entrance arches. It has the great

Veterans Wall and the Tribal Plaza, which will provide one of the greatest stadium entrances ever, in recognizing the history and tradition of the eleven tribes."

The new stadium will also include space for the University Marching Band, an "M" Room for alumni athletes and so much more. President Bruininks is also proud of the fact that the University has delivered on every promise made with regard to all aspects of the stadium and project funding.

"Not only did we raise the necessary 90 million dollars in private gifts to the University, but we also utilized the generosity of the donors in raising another 46 million dollars for academic scholarships, something we would not have achieved had it not been for the stadium fundraising efforts. It was very evident of the great caring that people have for academics at the University of Minnesota," says Bruininks.

"And Coach Brewster," says the president, "well, I am deeply appreciative of how he has connected to the high school coaches in the state and the community. He has hired a tremendous coaching staff, proven to be an outstanding recruiter, and really connected with local charity organizations. His overwhelming positive attitude and enthusiasm is far reaching and he has a real sense of citizenship. As we move into the new stadium, with one of the toughest football schedules in the nation ahead of us, Coach Brewster has us on the right track. Winning football games is next in the future for us."

Phil Esten, Associate Athletics Director at Minnesota, has been involved with the stadium project since 2003.

"September 12, 2009, will be a magical day with the opening of the new Gopher TCF Bank Stadium," says Esten. "It will be a Super Bowl type atmosphere."

Esten has been committed to the management of the stadium process for several years, and the excitement of opening the new home for the Gophers is evident in his every remark.

"There are two key stakeholders that we used to represent the importance of the planning process," says Esten. "The first are the fans and the students, and the second are the student athletes, but as equals in importance. It is the commitment of the University to make the game day experience for the fans and the students very special in every respect. Everything that was lost by the Gopher home field being off campus is back with the new stadium, and all of the important concepts that go with it. It is going to be a Big Ten experience for the fans and it is going to be a great atmosphere, collegiate and festive in every respect," says Esten.

The heritage of this great University and its competitive spirit certainly played a part in decisions about a new stadium. Minnesota is a member of one of the most competitive and legendary conferences in all of college football, the Big Ten conference. Sixteen times the Big Ten has sent six or more teams to college football bowl games, and conference teams are in the running for the country's top bowl games at the end of every football season.

In addition to receiving more national awards than any other conference, the Big Ten has had 15 winners of the coveted Heisman Trophy. Each year the Gophers compete for conference honors and recognition with other conference members representing the very best of competition.

With this phenomenal background and the great history behind the University of Minnesota, TCF Financial Corporation stepped forward to partner with the University by announcing a $35 million, 25-year corporate sponsorship for the new stadium. The partnership provides TCF with exclusive naming rights for the stadium, specifically to be called TCF Bank Stadium.

The total commitment for the new football stadium is $288.5 million, which includes the site preparation and the infrastructure improvements. A project of this magnitude takes incredible commitment, broad community support and major financial partners.

In addition to the TCF and University commitment, the balance of the funding comes from the state. Other significant funding includes a $10 million gift from the Shakopee Mdewakanton Sioux Community, a $2.5 million sponsorship agreement with Dairy Queen, $2.5 million in support from Best Buy and a $2 million gift from Target.

The effort to bring Gopher football back to campus has not just come from large corporate sponsorship, but also from many alumni and friends of the University of Minnesota. This has included gifts and sponsorships totaling over $75 million from close to 900 contributors.

The University's mission statement includes comments about the impact of the stadium. The section titled University Planning History

The new TCF Bank Stadium during construction during the spring of 2009.

includes the following:

"We will advance the University's fundamental academic mission. The University of Minnesota's fundamental academic mission in teaching, research, and public service is foremost and will be advanced. The mission of the institution will be preserved in all aspects of planning a multipurpose stadium. The future stadium development will not compromise the University's fundamental academic mission, purpose or programs."

With the concept in the early stages in 2003, the University initiated a feasibility study to determine the size and type of stadium, preliminary construction and operating costs, revenue potential and the various uses of the stadium beyond just football.

The planning was grounded in a set of guiding principles for the development of the on–campus stadium, which not only included the use of the stadium by the football team, but also for other University-related academic and athletic activities. With the support of the Board of Regents, the planning moved forward.

The strategy was to improve the financial circumstances of the University without presenting any financial risk to the academic mission.

Essentially the goal was to build the on-campus stadium with monies coming primarily from corporate and private donations and resources, without burdening the University and its overall mission.

The strategy also incorporated a plan to involve the neighboring community. The integration of the stadium into the area was extremely important to the University and project planners. The design plan and construction was to be compatible with all aspects of the campus environment and the surrounding commercial and residential neighborhoods. Respect for those working and living in the area was a critically important part of the project.

It was also important that the University be in control of the project in every respect. This included all phases of governance, design, development and ongoing management of the project.

The student experience and the intercollegiate athletic part of the project was another key area. The goal here was to have a major impact on the improvement of student life at the University. In addition the process was to increase enthusiasm in the community toward the University and to enhance the game day experience for everyone involved.

The feeling was that the new on-campus stadium environment would most certainly create many opportunities for University-wide events and celebrations that would lead to increased alumni and community support for the University of Minnesota. The venue will provide an incredible experience for fans and students attending the games and will enhance the football Saturdays for the players, coaches and all others associated

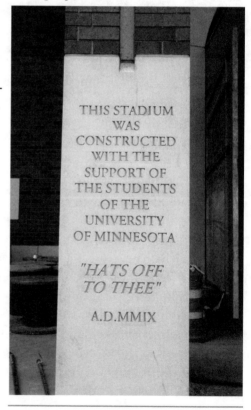

A pillar within the new stadium recognizes the support of the University students.

with the football program and community.

The infrastructure work began in June of 2006.

Coach Tim Brewster reports feeling goose bumps as he took part in the groundbreaking ceremony. Brewster is as excited as anyone as he takes his Gophers into their new home.

"It is awe inspiring," says Brewster about the stadium. "To have football back on campus again is really exciting!"

The primary architect on the project is Populous from Kansas City, Missouri, and they have been responsible for the stadium design. The new facility has retained some of the design elements present in Memorial Stadium.

The stadium will also include 39 suites, 59 loge boxes and 300 indoor club seats. The design configured the field of play in an east-west direction, distinguishing it from other Big Ten fields. This design will highlight the incredible campus views as well as the Minneapolis skyline.

"Populous didn't come to us with all kinds of plans telling us how the stadium should be built. They came to us with questions to determine what we wanted," said Associate Athletics Director Esten. "They have been great to work with. We visited all the Big Ten schools and several other stadiums around the country to pick the very best of each," says Esten. "The result is that we have a crown jewel."

"When recruits come in and see the stadium for the first time, it is nothing short of a jaw-dropping experience for them," says Esten. "The stadium without question cares about today but has not forgotten the past. The M Room honoring past Gopher letter winners is an indication of that commitment. The Marching Band Room salutes the band and its contributions to game days. The stadium will play host to more than football. It will be a multi-purpose facility. It will host concerts, physical education activities, recreational sports, high school sports such as football and soccer and will bring so much in the state together. It is truly an opportunity for the University to say thanks to the great state of Minnesota for the support," says Esten.

Jeff Spear, Myron Chase and Logan Gerken are Populous architects with primary responsibilities for the stadium. Their expertise and commitment to the project is inspiring.

"There is no other football stadium in the country like TCF Bank Stadium," says Jeff Spear. "The closest stadium to the design is the for-

The Gophers new locker room which will be second to none in the country.

mer Memorial Stadium."

The professional ownership for the project is evident as the three speak about the stadium and their relationship with the University of Minnesota and Mortenson Construction, the major contractors.

"Our relationship with the University and Mortenson has been outstanding. I cannot think of one single problem that has occurred," says Myron Chase. "They have been wonderful partners!"

TCF Bank Stadium will boast the third largest video board in all of college football. The scoreboard, credited to Daktronics, will have the latest in technology. The scoreboard, with dimensions of 48 feet high by 108 feet wide, is as large as the Golden Gopher basketball floor in Williams Arena.

Construction of the new football stadium officially began in July of 2007. Completion is scheduled for the summer of 2009, with the stadium ready for kick off on September 12, 2009, when the Golden Gophers host the Air Force.

The stadium's open-air horseshoe design will provide seating for 50,000, including general seating and an impressive number of premium type seats. A great deal of flexibility for expanding up to 80,000 seats has been built into the design,

Tom Wistrcill, Senior Associate Athletics Director, has an interesting take on the return to campus concept.

"We will all get to come back and be in college again," says Wistrcill. "We can come in early, stay late, and somewhere in the middle of everything, there will be a football game played. This will affect every part of the University of Minnesota. The various colleges within the University, the students, the faculty, the campus, the buildings, it will all be a part of the atmosphere. This is what it is all about!"

Marc Ryan, Associate Athletics Director, says that TCF Bank Stadium "goes far beyond just being a football stadium. It is obviously very important to the football team and the athletic department; however, it is also important to the University, the campus, the students, the community and the state of Minnesota and region. I truly believe there are fans who have been going to Gopher football games for many years and have never stepped foot on campus," says Ryan. "This is going to be different; a whole new exciting experience. It is going to be a day-long, or perhaps even a weekend long celebration, and will bring everything together again. Every part of the campus will be a part of the game day atmosphere. And at the end of the day, many will have shared in this incredible state asset."

"It is going to truly unify the community and bring everyone back together," says Betsi Sherman, Associate Marketing Director for the Gophers. "There has been almost a generation that has lost the campus atmosphere for Gopher football, and it is coming back. September 12, 2009, when the first game at TCF Bank Stadium is played, is going to be surreal. The pageantry and all that is going to be happening is going to be unbelievable. People have been waiting and waiting for so long and it is soon going to happen," says Sherman. "And with Coach Tim Brewster engaging everyone in such a positive way, he has made people start believing again. It is all going to be so incredible."

And there will be some other unique aspects of the stadium as it serves as the Gophers home. Described as a "Well Deserved Spot on the Roster," there will be a new home within the home just for letter winners at the University of Minnesota.

The M Room is quality space within TCF Bank Stadium for letter winners and their guests. This multipurpose area is 3000 square feet and is placed in a prime location. It is dedicated to all of the Golden Gopher athletes who have earned their legacy at the University of Minnesota. It is a place where they can gather with teammates and friends to create new memories, rekindle old histories, and continue to be a part of the Gopher tradition on game days and at events throughout the year.

The M Room is located on the ground level near the premium-seating lobby and the Hall of Fame area. The room will include a large meeting area with four flat panel televisions, a VCR/DVD player, a portable CD player and a sound system. The stadium's full kitchen will provide food service. The room will also include a private bar and private restrooms.

Some might question the building of an M Room within the new stadium. All of the dedication and pride that comes with earning the M is now rewarded by the granting of an official home, the M Room, as a belated thank you for the sacrifice and commitment of all Minnesota letter-winners.

George Adzick, Director of the "M" Club, is as excited as anyone for the Gophers to move into the new home. Adzick, a First Team All-Big Ten player for the Gophers in 1976 and drafted by the Seattle Seahawks, has been a tremendous leader for the "M" Club. His passion for Golden Gopher football and enthusiasm for involving former Minnesota letter winners has been appreciated by all. His desire to see the football Gophers back on campus is heartfelt.

"I walked east of Fourth Street between Mariucci Arena and Williams Arena and looked straight ahead and there was the new stadium. It was incredible. It seems as though it has always been there," says Adzick. "We will be able to hear the sounds of the game again, and we will be able to see the colors again. And we will be able to really hear the great Minnesota Marching Band again. It is going to be a great experience."

One of the most thrilling parts of Golden Gopher football throughout the years has been the incredible Minnesota Football Marching Band, which has entertained massive throngs at games for 116 years. The 300 member band, under the direction of Professor Tim Diem, has fired up the Gopher faithful with pre-game, halftime and post-game shows for over a century. The stadium has made available 20,000 square feet for the marching band to keep its extraordinary skills honed to perfection and to establish a permanent place for a University legacy.

Before the Gopher homecoming is complete, there is one final transition that has to take place: the great Gopher ghosts of the past have to make their move across the street and into their new home. You see, since 1992, when Memorial Stadium was torn down, they have had no resting place.

Since the move to the Metrodome in downtown Minneapolis, the legends have awaited a new home. Once Memorial Stadium was torn down, these ghosts have anticipated the opening of a new stadium. And finally the time has come.

So the ghosts of Gopher glory will have only a short distance to move and the memories that have kept Minnesota football alive since the last century will finally come home.

11

BREWSTER - A PASSION FOR ROSES

"We need to claim again what is rightfully ours. Before the others, it was us!"

He was right there as a youngster, right next to the Rose Bowl. There may be no other person who knows the setting better than Gopher Head Football Coach Tim Brewster.

"I know every square inch of that facility," says Brewster." I used to sneak in there and dream about the future. I used to lay right there on the middle of the field and look up at the sky and dream."

If you want passion and pride and tradition, well then, you have the right man. Tim Brewster has all of that and a lot more. And he is in the

Head Coach Tim Brewster leads the Golden Gophers onto the field.

right place at the right time as the head football coach for the Minnesota Golden Gophers football team.

An outstanding football player coming out of high school, Brewster was a hybrid wide receiver and tight end. He originally enrolled at Pasadena Community College and then was recruited to Illinois as a tight end, where he was a two-time selection as an All Big Ten player.

In 1984, his team of Fighting Illini went to the Rose Bowl, and Tim Brewster was team captain. He graduated from Illinois with a degree in political science. In 2008, the University of Illinois football program named him one of its ten greatest receivers of all time.

Brewster made an attempt at professional football, signing contracts with the New York Giants in 1984 and the Philadelphia Eagles in 1985. In 1986, he began his coaching career as a graduate assistant at Purdue University. When Coach Leon Burnett was fired mid-season, Brewster wound up selling cars for a short time. He learned quickly that sales was not the vocation for him.

It didn't take long, however, before he was hired as the head coach at Central Catholic High School in Lafayette, Indiana. He established a 15-8 record in two years and developed a wide-open passing attack, with his quarterback leading the state of Indiana in passing both years Brewster was head coach.

Desperately hoping to get into the college coaching ranks, Brewster drove to Chapel Hill, North Carolina, and convinced Mack Brown to hire him as an unpaid assistant for the 1989 season. Before the next season began, Brown hired him as the special teams coach, the tight ends coach and the recruiting coordinator.

Following the 1997 season, Brewster followed Brown to the University of Texas, where he served as tight ends coach from 1998-2001. He was also heavily involved in recruiting, landing some major prospects for the Longhorns.

After spending 13 years under Mack Brown, Brewster wanted to try professional football. In 2002 he was hired as the tight ends coach for the San Diego Chargers, where he worked for Marty Schottenheimer, long time NFL coach. In 2004, he was rewarded with the title of Assistant Head Coach. In 2005, he moved to the Denver Broncos as tight ends coach under Mike Shanahan.

After two years in Denver, Joel Maturi, Athletics Director at the

University of Minnesota, hired Tim Brewster to be the head football coach of the Golden Gophers. At his first press conference in the McNamara Alumni Center, Brewster announced his immediate goals were to "Win the Big Ten championship and take the Gopher Nation to the Rose Bowl."

The hiring process the University went through to hire Tim Brewster was quite the event. Once the decision was made to replace Coach Glenn Mason after the 44-41 loss to Texas Tech in the Insight Bowl concluding the 2006 season, Joel Maturi began his search for a new head coach.

Although the media attempted to be involved with every move, Maturi and his staff moved discretely and patiently. Associate Athletics Directors Marc Ryan and Tom Wistrcill were working with Maturi, putting together possible candidates and an analysis of what they wanted in a football coach to lead the Golden Gophers back to glory, not just for a season but for the long term.

They set about the process by engaging the assistance of Parker Executive Search Firm of Atlanta, Georgia.

"They did everything for us" says, Tom Wistrcill. "They arranged everything, which kept the process confidential for all those involved."

Maturi, Ryan and Wistrcill went to Atlanta with their list of potential candidates and met with the search firm, who then educated them on their database of coaches. Joel Maturi knew about Tim Brewster through his relationship with Minnesota Vikings coach Brad Childress. With this information and knowledge of Brewster's recruiting experience, as well as his tremendous football enthusiasm, the committee's interest heightened. It was also a big plus for Brewster that he had worked in great programs at Purdue, North Carolina and Texas. In the professional ranks he had learned under highly reputable mentors in Marty Schottenheimer and Mike Shanahan.

When the Minnesota search committee finished its work in Atlanta and returned to the University, there were ten candidates that they felt could possibly be successful as the Gophers' head coach. The final decision belonged to Joel Maturi, and it was very important to him that the coach have a plan for restoring Minnesota football to national prominence.

In order to avoid leaks about the process as well as the names of potential candidates, Parker Executive Search scheduled candidate interviews at hotels in Chicago and Dallas. Candidates would enter the hotel at their specific time, call Tom Wistrcill on his cell phone and be directed to meet Tom outside the elevator on the floor where the interviews were being held. Tom walked the candidate to the room and introduced him to Marc Ryan and Joel Maturi. Each candidate had a two and a half hour time slot for the interview, with a half hour in between so the candidates would not make any contact. The committee planned to interview six candidates in Chicago and four in Dallas.

"Brewster was incredibly prepared," said Wistrcill. "When we first met at the elevator, before we even got to the room, he mentioned to me that my father was a football coach. He knew my entire background. He did the same with Joel and Marc. He was really prepared and had done his homework on each of us."

"For me it was about recruiting," said Wistrcill, "and Brewster always seemed to bring recruiting into whatever was being discussed. He was extremely impressive."

"It was an exciting process and Tim Brewster was so prepared," says Marc Ryan. "He showed so much passion and energy, it was incredible. We knew so little about him at first, and he really hit the ground running in the interview. He had his coaches picked, knew how they would fit in, and spoke about each having great recruiting strengths. He was extremely impressive. The follow-up reference interviews were also so positive for him. His experience of working under great coaches like Mike Shanahan from the Denver Broncos, Marty Schottenheimer from the San Diego Chargers and Mac Brown at Texas was a great background, and each had such positive things to say about Tim Brewster."

After finishing the Chicago interviews, the committee flew to Dallas to meet the final four candidates. At the conclusion of the interviews, the candidate list was narrowed to two, and Tim Brewster and University of Florida defensive coordinator Charlie Strong were flown to the Twin Cities for more interviews, including a meeting with University President Robert Bruininks. It was determined soon after that Tim Brewster had become the leading candidate.

The search process involved a great deal of research into the candidates' previous coaching experience. The committee wanted to know details about candidates' recruiting practices, their coaching styles, their relationships with players and other coaches. Feedback on Tim Brewster was very positive. Brown, Schottenheimer and Shanahan all praised Brewster.

There was never a question in the mind of Shanahan that Brewster would make a great head coach.

"Tim has tremendous ability to relate to people," says Shanahan. "He has great communication skills, and I have absolutely no doubt that he will do amazingly well at the University of Minnesota. He is an outstanding recruiter and has a national reputation in this regard. He has landed some of the very top recruits when he was involved in college coaching," said Shanahan. "My son played at the University of Texas so I had the opportunity to watch Coach Brewster in action. He really stood

out. He has an incredible work ethic and drive, and is an excellent football coach. I went after him to coach with me in Denver because of what I saw in his work at Texas. He is going to study the Minnesota tradition and really embrace it."

Schottenheimer, former NFL head coach in Cleveland, Kansas City and San Diego, feels the same about Brewster.

"There are two things that are really important to me in a coach," says Schottenheimer. "The first is to have the ability to communicate with people and the second is to be a detail person. Coach Brewster is both of these and better at them than most. He has an outstanding way of communicating and is an outstanding detail person. He is a tremendous teacher and is great working with players. He will do exceptionally well with the Minnesota Gophers."

The next step in the process was for University of Minnesota administrators Kathy Brown and Joel Maturi to visit Brewster in Denver. Arrangements were made for them to stay at the Inverness Hotel, the same hotel the Denver Broncos stay at before home games.

After dinner, it was decided that the interviews would continue in Maturi's room at the Inverness, Room 261. As he approached the room, Brewster realized that Maturi was staying in the room where he always stayed with the Denver Broncos, Room 261. With over 1000 rooms available, Joel Maturi was given the same room that Brewster stays in.

What a coincidence.

The decision was made to hire Tim Brewster as the new head football coach at the University of Minnesota. He arrived in the Twin Cities two days later to meet the team.

"I told him I would pick him up at hotel at 6:00 a.m.," said Wistrcill. "I arrived about 5:50 a.m. and he was waiting for me. He was ready! The previous day I was scheduled to address the team about the head coaching status. I was to meet the team at 7:00 a.m. and at 6:55 I received the call from Joel Maturi that the decision was made on Brewster. With five minutes notice I told the team that Tim Brewster had been officially hired to be the new football coach. But we did our homework very carefully. Knowing that many of the squad would not likely have heard of

---

Brewster's ability to relate to and communicate with his players is one of his strengths.

Brewster, we prepared. Our two-time All-American center Greg Esslinger, who most of the team knew well, was now playing for the Denver Broncos, where Brewster was the tight ends coach. Esslinger's praise for Brewster was extraordinary. He said the players loved him, respected him, that he was a great coach and had tremendous enthusiasm and passion for coaching. With that ringing endorsement, the team was excited," said Wistrcill.

"The next morning, the second consecutive 7:00 a.m. meeting for the team, they awaited their new coach's arrival. Brewster approached the team, took off his jacket and he was something to watch," said Wisrcill. "After just a few seconds with their new coach, every guy in the room was ready to go out the door and hit someone. It was really something to see. It was as if he had prepared for that moment every day of the 23 years he had been in coaching. It was absolutely unbelievable. It was a special moment for all of us."

Tim Brewster has tremendous respect for people. He is an optimist in every possible way. He has studied the game of football for years and has tremendous passion for the game. Secondary to his family, football is his true joy. He developed his love for the game from the very first time he played.

He revels in the great tradition at the University of Minnesota and speaks proudly of the legendary figures like Bronko Nagurski, Bobby Bell and Carl Eller. He talks of the national championships won by the University of Minnesota, six of them, more than Ohio State, more than Michigan.

And in almost reverence, he speaks of Bernie Bierman winning five national championships at Minnesota, and of Bud Grant as perhaps the greatest all-around athlete to ever set foot on the University campus. Pride, passion, tradition, honor-they are embraced by Brewster as he looks to restore Minnesota football.

Brewster talks of his friend and former Gopher Tony Dungy.

"There is no greater man connected to the game of football than Tony Dungy," says Brewster. "He stands for greatness and I feel like he is watching me to be sure I live life the way it should be lived. He has

---

Brewster spent 13 years working under Mack Brown at North Carolina and Texas before making the jump to coaching in the NFL.

character and is a real man with high morals and he was such a great coach," says Brewster. "I want Tony Dungy to be proud of our University of Minnesota football team."

And Brewster wants the fans and the students to be proud of the football team again. He wants to reach out to the students and have them become the 12th man on the field. He wants football to be important on campus.

"Playing football on campus is a huge advantage to the home team," says Brewster, "and we have it again. And I know what it takes to win a Big Ten championship. I have been a part of it. I know what it takes to go to the Rose Bowl and I have been a part of that also."

Brewster knows that a team can turn its fortunes around in quick fashion. He is the first to recall Coach Murray Warmath's 1960 Gopher team.

"The 1959 team finished last in the Big Ten and the 1960 team under Warmath won the national championship. That turnabout is the greatest story in the history of college football," exclaims Brewster. "It can be done!"

There is no question that for Coach Brewster football success is more than just winning. It also entails all of the things that go along with the college football experience: the game day atmosphere, the sportsmanship involved in the game, and the respect for the game. He believes coaches convey this respect to their players, and that it includes respecting your opponent. He believes Saturdays must be special for the fans, the students, the players, the coaches, the administrators and all those who are connected to the game and present to enjoy the game day experience.

"Being the head football coach at the University of Minnesota is more than I ever expected," says Coach Brewster. "I love the history and the tradition of the Golden Gophers. I love the players and their families, and I have a tremendous responsibility that comes with the stewardship of this program. And I am driven to make it special again."

"The tradition that goes with this program is also more than I ever thought when I first took the job. Great players like Bobby Bell and Carl Eller are such a big part of the past," says Brewster. "There has been so much pain around for so many years due to the team's lack of success. It has been there and it is extremely hurtful for many of the former players."

Former players like Bobby Bell have delivered tremendous support for the Gopher program.

"I talk to Bobby Bell all the time," says Brewster. "He has been an unbelievable presence for us."

And Bobby Bell has never forgotten what the University of Minnesota has meant to him.

"Coach Tim Brewster has my 100% percent support for the Gopher program," says Bell. "He has that fire inside him and I would love to play for him."

Bell's trips to the campus from his Kansas City home are proof of his support for the program and Coach Brewster.

Brewster believes that the team and the program are on the right track.

"Everywhere I go I meet people who are supporting me and the program and who believe that we are going to win again," says Brewster. "Take a person like Bob McNamara, who does so much for the program and who was such a great player of the past, truly one of the greatest athletes to ever wear the maroon and gold. No one wants to win more than Bob McNamara. No one."

There also is a strong commitment by the coach to do everything possible to keep the elite Minnesota high school football player at home. For the coach, loyal fans and alumni, it is disheartening to see some of the best homegrown talent going elsewhere.

"I really appreciate the reaching out to high school coaches in the state that Coach Brewster has done," says Mike Grant, highly successful football coach at Eden Prairie High School. "He has brought in a tremendously high energy level and shown his workaholic nature. He has worked tirelessly in making contact with the high school coaches and has held football clinics, which have been very important. The new stadium is going to really help," says Grant, "and the fact that Gopher football will be back on campus again is going to be huge for recruiting."

Grant has been impressed with what Coach Tim Brewster has brought to Gopher football.

"He is not afraid to show that he is learning in the job," says Grant. "Changing the offensive philosophy is a good example of that. With the way college football is changing because of the television coverage and the attention given to all aspects of the game, it's not the same anymore. And with Coach Brewster's enthusiasm, his reaching out to the coaches, the new stadium and football back on campus, there are going to be some exciting times ahead," says Grant.

Another of the legendary coaches in Minnesota high school history who is impressed with the job Brewster is doing is Don Swanson. Swanson played college football at Gustavus Adolphus College and coached at Patrick Henry in Minneapolis for 28 years.

"I am really impressed with Coach Brewster," says Swanson. "He is a good man and I like the attitude he brings to the Gophers. He loves to talk to the high school coaches in the state and he listens to what they have to say. And you know what else, they believe in him. He also is really active with the clinics and this is huge with the high school coaches because it shows how much he is interested in what they do."

Swanson is also a strong believer in what the new stadium will mean to recruiting.

"It puts us on a level playing field with the others who are recruiting against us," he says. "It is really going to be something!"

Brewster fully understands that success won't come easy. As he says, the proof is in the pudding.

"But we have taken the proper steps," says the coach, "and we are building from the ground up."

Brewster is also committed to academic success for his players. He demands class attendance and solid work in the classroom. He will tell you about the academic achievements of his players as often as he will talk about wins. It is important to him and he never stops thinking about it.

"When I came to Minnesota, I developed a gold ring with a maroon "M" on it," says Brewster. "It is specially made for each player who earns a football letter, and it will be given to the player when he graduates."

Brewster also developed an incentive for his players to go to class.

"If any player misses a class the entire team will gather the next morning at 6:00 a.m. and they will run," says Brewster. "And after they get done running, the player who missed class will get up in front of all of them and tell the team that they all ran because he missed class. It is a pretty good incentive to attend class," says the coach.

Brewster is very proud when he announces that his squad had more

Academic All-Big Ten players than any team in the conference. Brewster has it figured out. He knows the importance of thriving both on the field and in the classroom.

Brewster also clearly knows that building a successful program starts with recruiting. It starts with understanding program tradition and communicating that this is not just another football program, but rather a football program that has won six national championships and 18 Big Ten titles. The team has a history of outstanding players. The Twin Cities is a special place to live and to go to school. The University of Minnesota is one of the country's great research universities.

There must be an understanding throughout the state that the Gopher football program wants the best players in the state to come to Minnesota. It is important that high school coaches, athletes and parents understand this.

The tradition of honoring the great players of the past must always be kept in focus.

"Take Bobby Bell," says Brewster. "He will always be such a big part of our program. My favorite team growing up was the Kansas City Chiefs, and I used to wear number 78 as a youngster because that was Bobby Bell's number. I believe he was the greatest defensive player of all time. And we have to remember others like Bud Grant, who I talk about often. Bud might have been the most celebrated and decorated athlete to ever step on to this campus. He won nine letters while at Minnesota, which is incredible," says Brewster.

Coach Brewster wants players of great character. He wants players who understand passion and tradition. He wants players who excel both on and off the field. Players on his teams have to know what it means to put on the maroon and gold uniform and be a Golden Gopher football player.

"As the head football coach, I try to get to know the young men," says Brewster. "I want to know that they are all together, academically, physically and spiritually."

***

Dan O'Brien is the Director of Football Operations under Head Coach Tim Brewster and gets an up-close look at how Coach Brewster operates daily. Dan was the athletic director at Hamline University for six years prior to joining the Gophers and previously was at Concordia from 1995-2002. Dan was an All-Minnesota Intercollegiate Athletic Conference player as a defensive back at the University of St. Thomas, where he also served as team captain for two seasons.

O'Brien grew up loving Golden Gopher football.

"I can remember as a youngster being out in the yard raking leaves and listening to the Gopher games on the radio," says O'Brien. "It was very special. I'm a Minnesota guy and to do what I do at the only Division I school, to be the Director of Football Operations for the Gophers, it's a great honor. I am thankful to be a part of the Gopher football program. Working in the capacity that I do for Gopher football keeps me excited everyday."

"Working for Coach Brewster is an incredible experience. He has tremendous energy and always stays positive. The stress and pressure that he is under is unbelievable but at the end of the day, he is always treating people well. He is very family centered. Coach Brewster wants our families to be a part of all of this and welcomes us to bring our wives and children around the program," says O'Brien. "Being in the kind of work that we are in is not a job, it is a lifestyle and I am proud to be a part of it."

O'Brien's responsibilities are numerous. He must ensure that operations run smoothly. This includes travel, hotels and food service, as well as many other day-to-day operational activities.

O'Brien has a great reputation and is easy to work with. He truly likes what Coach Brewster stands for when working with the athletes.

"Coach Brewster is always looking to recruit the very best players and best individuals in the country. He makes a run at the best. He wants great athletes, good character people and competitive personalities," says O'Brien. "He looks at each one of his players like he is one of his own. He takes great pride in getting to know them. They are that important to him."

"Coach Brewster is looking for kids that have the competitive spirit. He wants those that know how to win and know how to play in the close games. He wants those that know how to play the game when they are behind. The coach wants the player who doesn't want to just get through a practice/workout session, but rather the kid who wants to win the Big Ten championship on the practice field. He wants leaders on the team. He looks for loyalty, a terrific work ethic, great attitudes and competitive skills," says O'Brien.

"Coach Brewster's greatest strength is that he genuinely believes the Minnesota Gophers will go to the Rose Bowl."

There is no doubt that Brewster is the kind of coach that Dan O'Brien wants to be around; he trusts him and he believes in him. And the Gopher football program is fortunate to have a person like Dan O'Brien as a part of the program, bringing his passion, loyalty and commitment to the Golden Gophers every day.

***

Meghan Potter is the Assistant to the Head Coach.

"There is never a dull moment being around Coach Brewster," says Meghan. "Every day is a good day working for him. He treats everyone in a first class manner all the time. Even after a tough loss, he is always positive and after a win, he is so pumped up!"

Meghan Potter was an 11th and 12th grade English teacher and is currently pursuing a degree in Sports Management at the University of Minnesota. She is a perfect fit for the position, being actively involved in the football program. She has a wonderful personality and is always helpful to everyone. It is obvious she loves her job working for the head football coach.

"Coach Brewster is 100% real. He is exactly what you see," says Potter. "If I were to describe him, I would have to say the words would be passionate, enthusiastic, dynamic, hard-working, confident and driven. There is nothing fake about him. He is always searching for a better way to do things and everything he does is right from the heart."

Coach Tim Brewster is likely as excited as anyone about getting the Golden Gophers football team back on campus. The September 12, 2009 game against the Air Force at the new TCF Bank Stadium is going to be an extraordinary event, and a day that will always be remembered.

"It's the missing piece," says Brewster. "It brings it all together."

The plan is in place and the stadium is going to be a big factor. The wins are going to come more regularly than the losses.

"Last season, we sang the rouser seven times after those seven wins," says Brewster "and it's a lot more fun winning."

The coach's philosophy is that after a loss, there is no time to spend feeling bad. He has to get ready for the next week's game.

"Last year we were the biggest turnabout in the country going from one win the previous season to seven wins, and we have to build on that," says Brewster.

***

Six national championship seasons. Incredible teams of the past. Phenomenal players of yesterday and a new football stadium second to none. It has been too long and it is time for a Golden Gophers return to prominence. With the opening of TCF Bank Stadium and the Minnesota Golden Gophers football team back on campus, smelling roses may be in the near future.

Last fall, Meghan Potter was the go-between for a regular yet rather unusual occurrence. After every Gopher win, a rose was delivered to Coach Brewster's office from an anonymous source, with a card which reported the score of the game and contained the following the message: "One step closer."

And if you enjoy the odd twist of fate, then consider that Tim Brewster was born in the year 1960. 1960 was also the year the Gophers won their last national championship. Do you suppose that is an omen from the football gods? You never know!

Minnesota Golden Gopher football holds a special place in the hearts of the faithful. It is over a century old and filled with so much glory and so much pride. The players, the coaches, the alumni, and the great fans of the past, present and future are now coming home to the new TCF Bank Stadium to embrace a new era of Gopher football.